# Mother from Hell

KEN & PATRICK DOYLE were born and raised in Tullamore, Co. Offaly. The story of the horrific abuse they suffered at the hands of their own mother was first revealed in the *Sunday World* newspaper. Ken now lives in the US and Patrick in the UK.

# Mother from Hell

Two Brothers. A Sadistic Mother.
A Childhood Destroyed.

KEN & PATRICK DOYLE

WITH NICOLA PIERCE

THE O'BRIEN PRESS
DUBLIN

First published 2009 by The O'Brien Press Ltd.
12 Terenure Road East, Dublin 6, Ireland.
Tel: +353 1 4923333; Fax: +353 1 4922777
E-mail: books@obrien.ie
Website: www.obrien.ie
Reprinted 2009 (twice).

ISBN 978-1-84717-143-6



British Library Cataloguing-in-Publication Data
A catalogue record for this title is available from the British Library

3 4 5 6
09 10 11 12 13

Editing, typesetting and design: The O'Brien Press Ltd
Printed by Cox & Wyman Ltd.

# CONTENTS

Introduction 9

Prologue 13

Part One: Ken

The First Time 19

Hail Mary 21

Hunger 30

Neighbourhood Watch 41

'A Woman's Work' 49

Robber Doyles 57

'Cheese Please!' 73

Part Two: Patrick

Runaway 93

'My Days Were Numbered' 105

Crossing The Irish Sea 112

'My Present, My Future, My World' 118

'Mad Irishman' 128

My Own Family 132
Home For The Holidays 135
An Expensive Habit 139
Mental Cruelty 142
The Last Straw 149
No Escape 155

Part Three: Ken

Running From The Past 161
St Joseph's 170
Crime Spree 177
A New Life 190
Betrayed By The System 202
Reunited 211

Part Four: Patrick

Living With Post-Traumatic Stress Disorder 217
Afterword 227
Appendix 229
It Shouldn't Hurt To Be A Child 253

# Acknowledgements

Firstly I want to thank all the staff at the *Sunday World* newspaper. Thanks to them I was reunited with my big brother Patrick after twenty-two years. They'll never know how much it meant to us that they supported us from the very beginning and published our story of abuse.

A big 'thank you' to everyone in Ireland who helped us to access our files through the Freedom of Information Act 1997, thus providing us with the hard evidence that we needed.

I also want to thank Dr David B. Wohlsifer and Dr Berman at Bala Psychological Resources, in Bala Cynwyd, Pennsylvania, who are both helping me cope with my post-traumatic stress disorder (PTSD). I don't think I'd be around today if it wasn't for their counselling and support.

**Ken Doyle, 2009**

✠ ✠ ✠

I would like to thank the following people for all their help and unflagging support in getting me to this point of my life:

My doctor, John Rees, Ravenhill, Swansea, and all his friendly staff.

Drs Millington and Bradley at the same surgery, along with Dr Liz Jackson at Pen-A-Byrn Surgery, in Gorseinon, Swansea;

*The Sunday World* for breaking the story all the way back in 2002;

My wife Bernadette who has stood by me for all the years of trouble and strife;

Our wonderful family of four daughters and three sons;

Last, but not least, I would like to thank Mr Michael O'Brien and all the staff at The O'Brien Press for publishing our story.

**Patrick Doyle, 2009**

# Introduction

In 1824 Richard Martin MP ('Humanity Dick') helped found the Society for the Prevention of Cruelty to Animals, the first national animal protection society in the world. The Dublin branch of this UK society opened less than twenty years later and is today the largest animal welfare organisation in Ireland. Jump forward another twenty-plus years, across the ocean to 1880s New York, where a woman hears a child in obvious distress. When she goes to help it the child's own mother blocks her way. Undeterred the woman goes into a police station to enlist their help, but they shake their heads and tell her that it's none of their business. Still the woman is determined to do something although, when she considers them, she notes that her options are quite limited. Then she realises what she must do. She contacts the Society for the Prevention of Cruelty to Animals and tells them that an animal is being mistreated at such and such address. An inspector is immediately despatched to the scene. Presumably he is more than a little surprised to find not a cat nor a dog, but a young child in need of help.

Nevertheless the case ends up in Court and the mother is charged with cruelty to an animal. A short while later the first Society for the Prevention of Cruelty to Children (SPCC) is founded – at long last.

Is it easier to report that an animal is being abused than it is to report a child in the same circumstances? If this is the case is it because an animal clearly cannot tell anyone about its suffering while the neighbour, the teacher, the relative would much prefer the child to speak up and report the abuse him or herself? The thing is, however, and this is certainly relevant in the story of Patrick and Kenneth's dreadful childhood, the abused child loves or fears its mother, as only a child can; either way it doesn't want to get her into any trouble.

In one sense Patrick and Kenneth are lucky; they lived to tell their tale. In another sense they didn't really live, not in the fullest sense of the word; they merely survived. And that is what they continue to do today. One is a grandfather, while the other is a self-confessed loner, and despite the fact that they took very different paths in adulthood, the legacy of their mother's abuse in their normal day-to-day lives – in Swansea for Patrick and in New Jersey for Ken – is strewn with many absolute similarities. Fifty years on and the two boys-or men-are possibly still as trapped as they always were thanks to the post-abuse onslaught of Post Traumatic Stress Disorder.

They also share another condition: pure outrage at those who failed them.

A few years ago, prompted by his American doctors, Ken

applied for his medical files and was devastated to discover something that neither he nor his brother ever suspected; the authorities knew about their abuse. Page after page of opinions, some of which can be found at the back of this book, were filed away to gather dust while the two boys were left to continue being battered and starved in their Tullamore home. Following a lacklustre confrontation with their mother and father Patrick and Ken took their story to the front page of the *Sunday World*, making the unenviable decision to expose their mother and her brutality – as well as themselves – to the nation. Their story appeared on 1 September 2002, under the headline, 'This Is The Most Evil Mum in Ireland'.

This is a story of Ireland in the sixties and seventies, and unfortunately it is also a story of Ireland today. As this book goes to press a forty-year-old Roscommon mother of six begins a seven-year prison sentence for neglect and ill-treatment of her children, including forcing her barely teenaged son to have sex with her. The judge, who presided over the case, states how the six malnourished, lice-ridden and unwashed children were 'failed by everyone around them'.

Of course it's not just an Irish story. Only last year an Austrian father was arrested for holing up his daughter in secret chambers beneath his house to rape her whenever he felt like it. Across the water in the UK a toddler finally died at the hands of his mother, her boyfriend and their lodger, despite numerous visits from social workers.

What do the two Doyles hope to achieve with this book? They were both advised to write down their experience by their doctors. Therefore what you read between these covers is partly therapeutic homework, partly hopeful attempt to begin exorcising some of their demons. Mostly the brothers want to add their voices to those who have gone before them and speak up for those who haven't managed to yet do so. The main question posed by this book, and by the Doyle brothers, is why? Why are people hurting or killing babies, toddlers, six year olds? Why is it happening so often? Why aren't more questions asked when a child is constantly hungry, bruised, or smells so bad that the other kids in its class refuse to hold its hand? Why are social workers and the health boards not able to do more to help? Why are we, as a race, so bloody careless, or polite, when it comes to the lives of children? Why?

# Ken's Prologue

She met me at the back door, her face set in a dreadful pose of something between pure rage and madness. Her weapon of choice, the dreaded 'Cheese Please!' board was in her right hand, her sleeves were rolled up to the elbow and her large body tensed in preparation for what she felt she must do. I stared at her stupidly as she towered over me; I had been in school all day and could not think of a single reason for this horrible welcome home. All my classmates were probably entering their own houses at this exact moment, to be greeted by their smiling mothers who perhaps handed them a glass of milk and a sandwich, telling them to do their homework before putting on the TV. I was very sure that none of them, at this moment in time, were in actual fear for their lives. Suddenly she lunged forward, grabbing me by my shirt and ripping it from my body. Next it was my trousers, shoes, socks and pants. By the time I was naked we were in the middle of the kitchen and my fate was sealed.

Apparently I had robbed my sister's purse. This was today's reason. She started to whack me around my back and shoulders with the board, kicking my legs from under me, all the while explaining that my sister had visited that morning and now her purse was gone, and I had obviously taken it. In between my yelps of pain I tried to argue that I couldn't have possibly taken it as I had been in school, that I had absolutely no idea my sister had been visiting her, but it was pointless. It was always utterly pointless. She dragged me off the floor, from where I was cowering beneath the steady rhythm of blows to my upper body, and into the living room, tossing me carelessly into an armchair. Through my tears and pain I watched her bind my legs and arms to the chair using pairs of her nylon tights before tying a tea towel around my mouth to gag me. The real beating was about to commence.

And, as usual, no one would hear my muffled screams.

# Patrick's Prologue

Most nights I find myself plagued by the same recurring dream. I see a little girl, with stringy brown hair, dirty face, who's maybe two or three years of age. She's dressed in a white dress and tights and is standing in her cot which I happen to notice is full of urine and excrement. When she sees me she starts to cry, calling out to me, heavy tears running down her face, wanting me to help her. I'm horrified by her predicament and quickly rush to lift her out of the filth, but just as I'm about to grab her she vanishes.

I've been having this dream for years.

# Part One:

# Ken

1969 TWO OF THREE

**NOTES**

REGISTER NO.................. FRIEND'S ADDRESS ..................

(2)

31. XII. 69.
Vomited once tonight
Father says that child is neglected — only getting one meal / day

O/E T° 101·5°F P. 120/min
Child emaciated — not dehydrated
Quite an intelligent little boy.

Abdomen: H.S.√ Tongue moist.
Bowels okay.
pot-belly
No masses or [illegible] Chest clear No cough or chest colds
No glands D. Malnutrition — neglect

DIET... [illegible]

| DATE | TREATMENT (Including Extra Diet and Stimulants) | DATE | TREATMENT (Including Extra Diet and Stimulants) |
| --- | --- | --- | --- |
| | Rx Food ++ | | |
| | Vitamins | | |
| | [illegible] | | |
| | 1. Weigh → 27½ lb | | |
| | 2. X-Ray: Chest | | |
| 5/1/70 | 2nd, 3rd toes on lt. side are infected — blistering. [illegible] powder | | |
| [illegible]/1/70 | [illegible] Home [illegible] | | |
| | [illegible] | | |
| [illegible] | next clinic | | |

FILM DATE please

(B)

# The First Time

*'[Your father] outlines how he ... sought help from Social Workers, District Nurse/Health Officer, a Doctor and other health professionals but it never arrived. He places a large proportion of blame on the Health Boards for lack of action and support.'*

(14 November 2003 – An Garda Síochána)

My brother Patrick remembers my first beating, of which I assume I was completely unaware. He was just five years old when he watched our mother punching herself again and again in her pregnant stomach while shouting at the top of her voice,

'I don't want this fucking child!'

Which was me. My father told her to calm down, that having a baby was something natural and anyway she couldn't stop it from happening now. In response she screamed obscenities at the bump, until Patsy, my father, lost his temper and told her to shut up in case the neighbours heard. With that she marched over to the window, opened it and bellowed out for anyone to hear that the neighbours did not pay her rent – whatever that meant. My father reacted in his customary way, he told her she was sick and took himself off to the pub in disgust. As soon as he closed the door behind him she began to wail, calling me, the unborn foetus, all sorts of dreadful names, punctuating her diatribe with several more hard thumps to her belly.

I cannot say that I remember this, but it was certainly a hard thing to forget once I was told about it. Imagine someone hating you before you are even born. Does that make it more personal or less so? It would appear that no matter how I turned out, or whatever I looked like, I never had a chance for her love.

When I was a year old, my father's parents reported their daughter-in-law to the Irish Society For the Prevention of Cruelty to Children (ISPCC) in Athlone. The year was 1965 and six-year-old Patrick was caught stealing food from people's bins because his mother often did not allow him to eat or drink. They also saw his scrawny and badly bruised back, after a recent beating when my father, utterly bewildered, rushed Patrick around to their house so that they could tend to the cuts with iodine and cotton wool. From what we can piece together the only consequence was war in our house, and all us children were banned from ever visiting our grandparents again. If anybody asked us any questions our only answer was to be, 'I don't know'. My father's sister, our beloved Aunt Tess, who lived in America, got on a plane and flew home to beg Patrick to return to the States with her where she promised to take care of him. He refused; saying he didn't want to leave his mother. After all, what six-year-old does?

# Hail Mary

*'Kenneth Doyle ... urgent need for this boy to be removed from home ... Many signs of parental rejection, at present want him out of the home.'*
(Midland Health Board, 3 March 1976)

Neither of us knows a lot about our mother Olive. She was born and bred in Dublin, one of six children, and did not seem particularly close to her family. Her mother died when she was young and she was raised by an older sister. Her father worked for CIE, the national transport company. Certainly, my father wasn't close to his in-laws.

When he drove us up to Dublin for our infrequent visits to family members, he merely dropped us off before continuing on to the pub, picking us up when we were ready to go home after the allotted hour – which was how long he allowed her to stay. Both Patrick and I hated one particular relative of my mother's. Thanks to Olive's lying tales about us the feeling was pretty much mutual. On one visit, Patrick overheard a conversation about us; as usual we were being described as 'demons', who never gave poor Olive a minute's peace. The relative's advice was to deprive us of food, 'That will make them learn!';

the words were put into action – the table was set for lunch, the others were called in, and Patrick and I were sent out to the back garden for the duration of the meal.

Before her marriage Olive worked at the John Player's cigarette factory in Phibsboro, Dublin. I cannot tell you anything about where or when she met our father. I don't even remember ever seeing a photograph of their Dublin wedding, although Patrick does recall an old black and white photograph that was kept in an album, in which Olive appears as a young, slim, tall, good-looking girl on the arm of her handsome be-suited new husband. They are both smiling with happiness, as most couples do on their wedding days when they are on the threshold of an exciting new beginning, a new life to be faced together through the good times and bad. If someone had told that radiant young bride that within the next five years she would be terrorising and starving two of her own children, I wonder what she would have said.

When Patrick was born in 1958 the family – my parents and oldest sibling, who was then about three years old – were living in the UK, in Brixton. Shortly afterwards, my parents decided to move back to my father's home town of Tullamore in Offaly, where I was born in 1964.

It's a nice place, Tullamore, (or '*An Tulach Mhór*', which means 'The Big Hill') and has undergone many, many changes since I was a young boy. The town, which is the most central town in Ireland, with a population of approximately 20,000, was founded in AD 553 by Saint Columba and is today a popular place for tourists, owing to the likes of Srah Castle, which was built in 1588 by John Briscoe, who was an officer in Queen Elizabeth's army. My brother Patrick spent many a night in this castle, whose cold, dark, roofless ruins were infinitely preferable to staying at home. During the latter half of the sixteenth century the counties of Laois and Offaly were 'planted' by English families who came over to bulk up the population of Ireland with 'gentlemen and women'; these initial residents were known as the 'Elizabethan Planters'. There is a second castle, which was designed by celebrated architect, Francis Johnston, in the turbulent year of 1798, but not built until the early 1800s. Charleville Castle is reputed to be one of the grandest examples of Gothic revival architecture in the country. Last, but by no means least, there is the infamous Tullamore Jail, whose most famous resident might well have been the County Cork nationalist, journalist and author William O'Brien, founder of the United Irish League in 1898. Later on, the jail became 'home' to angry republicans during the brutal civil war, which erupted after the battle that was Ireland's War of Independence (1919-1921).

Tullamore also claims to be the location of the world's first aviation disaster. In 1785 a hot air balloon crashed somewhere near the area of Patrick Street, igniting a huge fire which caused widespread destruction. But perhaps Tullamore is most famous for its whiskey, Tullamore Dew, which was first distilled in 1829, and named after owner Daniel E. Williams (DEW), who lived in Dew Park. The distillery closed in the 1950s and the whiskey is now produced by Irish Distillers

Ltd., in Midleton, County Cork.

Who knows what Olive made of her new home? She was not exactly a sociable woman and never seemed to have any friends. Patsy's parents lived nearby, but that would have provided little comfort. My grandfather later confided in Patrick that they had begged their son not to marry her, and it was they whose hearts were broken by her treatment of us, after those few and far between times when they had been able to see us. Following the 1965 call to the ISPCC they were no longer welcome in our home and even Patsy could only visit them on his wife's say so. She never ever forgave them and would spend a lot of time running them down in front of us children, telling horrible fictional stories about them and calling them unspeakable names. One time she told us that our grandmother, a devout woman, was having an affair with the local priest. Of course, like most of the things she told us, it was a preposterous lie.

She hardly left the house, except to get her short, brown hair permed once a week, to do some shopping, or maybe to make the odd expedition to play Bingo. Perhaps she only relaxed within the walls of her own home. Her loathing of the neighbours seemed heightened by her paranoia that they were either full of themselves and spent their time looking down their noses at her, or were her superior in a material world; all of her own making. For instance, if she heard any of the other women outside on the street we were instructed to spy out the window and provide her with a detailed description of their hairstyle and wardrobe. Whatever they were wearing she immediately wanted a more expensive version for herself.

Like many full-time housewives of the time her interests were few beyond listening to Gay Byrne on his morning radio programme, Monday to Friday, and watching him present his *Late, Late Show* on a Saturday night. Another favourite was *The Riordans*, an Irish soap opera similar to the British *Emmerdale*. The only reading she did was the weekly *Tullamore Tribune*, which she trawled through hoping to find out any gossip about who was arrested or up in court that week. She enjoyed the Sunday outings to mass when she would dress up in all her finery, before taking *her* seat – which was the very front seat – in church, at least thirty minutes before the ceremony was due to begin; I suppose this was to ensure the availability of the front pew. There she would sit, looking as holy as you like, threading her rosary beads through her fingers. She had a particular fondness for Padre Pio, the Italian priest who, for fifty years, physically bore the five wounds of the crucifixion. People would pray to him if there was a sickness in the family. Olive's handbag was usually crammed with religious paraphenalia: rosary beads, prayer books, relics and little cards of Padre Pio and other saints which she would present to people, advising them on the choice of prayers – usually multiple 'Hail Marys' – that they should recite for a specific number of nights, which would send their troubles packing. At home, after mass, she would ridicule the priest and the various neighbours she had cheerily greeted and chatted with outside the church. She harboured a deep dislike for other people and needed us as an audience for her bitter expositions of the local community.

When Patrick was five years old his brown-eyed mother loved nothing better than to hold the red hot poker up to his face, threatening to brand him. Rearing herself up to her full height she would roar at him, as if the frightened child was old Satan himself,

'Pull in your horns, Nick.'

'I will, Mammy, I will.'

The immense heat and proximity of the poker made his eyes tear up and he feared she would poke the burning stick into his ear or into his mouth. Again she would scream at him words he didn't understand.

'You're a devil. I said pull your horns in! Remove thy vein from thy head.'

The interior of our house was also evidence of her religious leanings. Aside from the pictures of Saint Joseph, and ironically enough Our Lady, Mary the – presumably kind and loving – Mother of God, that were dotted around the hall and landing, there was also, in the kitchen, one of those large framed pictures of the Sacred Heart of Jesus, which was lit up by a four inch cross that glowed from inside a plastic casing. Patrick grew to hate this piece when it became the focus of a particular punishment, whereby she made him strip to his birthday suit and kneel in front of it, all the while telling God aloud over and over again that he was ugly and scum. Not too surprisingly Patrick does not talk much to God today. In his child's mind God was her willing accomplice. For my part whenever I received a beating in the kitchen, a common location, I was alerted to the fact that a particular session had finished only when she turned to the Sacred Heart and blessed herself, perhaps thanking the Creator for having had the strength to beat the living daylights out of me. She would also make me stand and regard the picture while telling me that she hoped very much that God would strike me down and that I was 'a dying-looking bastard', which was one of her favourite terms of 'endearment' for me.

Patsy, on the other hand, had lots of friends in the town. I suppose he would have grown up with some of them or knew them from school. He was also close to his family, in spite of his wife, and regularly went fishing with his cousin. He could turn his hand to most things and could do anything about the house, from welding, roofing and building to the actual wiring and heating. In fact he enjoyed nothing better than renovating the house, when he wasn't constructing model boats and planes from the Airfix box sets. I'm sure that Olive must have been envied by the neighbours for her comfortable house and talented husband; as much as I'm sure that she had not one iota of appreciation for either of them. Another hobby of his was photography and he took hundreds of photos with good quality cameras.

My father wasn't what you would call a strong man. At times his heavy drinking led to short bouts of violence, but perhaps he was provoked beyond endurance. At any rate, he had plenty of drinking companions as there was not much else in the town, during the sixties, by way of entertainment. He also often helped out the local Gardaí by performing security at the big football matches.

Things might have been very different for Patrick and me

had our father found regular employment in Tullamore. Instead he decided to go to America in search of work. I don't know how hard, or easy, a decision this was for him. I have a suspicion that Patsy, more than anything else, just wanted to enjoy his life. More importantly he had the ability to. You meet so many people today who are miserable for one reason or another and they genuinely don't know what would make them happy, or even just happier. Patsy had no problem working hard, but he also liked to make time for his models, fishing, driving his friends to golf courses, plus drinking with his different crowds of mates. You have to wonder how much the increasing unpleasantness of his married life had to do with his decision to go so far away for work. There were no computers in those days, and therefore no emails to keep in touch. We didn't even have a phone in the house in those days. Accordingly America seemed to be a very long way from Tullamore indeed. Frequent contact was maintained through his letters, which were always accompanied by dollars. Olive never wanted for money; Patsy made sure that she had everything she needed, which only makes her behaviour towards us even more incredible.

As it was, he packed up his bags and over the next few years we only saw him at Christmas time when he would come home for a month-long visit. Olive had us all to herself and that's when things got really serious. She was usually pregnant by the time he got the plane back to the States and by 1969 she was five months pregnant, with seven children under the age of fourteen. It can't have been easy, I appreciate that, but nothing can excuse the utter savagery that was unleashed in between my father's visits. At the time we assumed our father was completely ignorant of how things were in his absence, and we were much too frightened, or maybe it would be more honest to say that we were much too depressed, to tell him anything on his annual visits.

# Hunger

*'I have spoken to Sister X who was the social worker involved with the family. She feels that Mrs Doyle in particular is very plausible but with time it becomes obvious that her recounting of different situations can be at variance with what actually happened.'*

(Social Worker's Report, undated)

Olive was quite a big woman who enjoyed her food, in large quantities. After a typically substantial meal she would stand up and put her hands on her wide hips, turn herself sideways and ask us all if we thought she had put on weight, to which she received a resounding 'No!' for a reply. Our answer never varied. For some reason, however, she didn't like Patrick and me to eat or drink. And so we mostly didn't. I was a sickly baby from the very beginning, being born premature at thirty-five weeks following months of haemorrhaging for Olive – not too surprising considering how she used to punch her pregnant belly. When I was four or five years old I was admitted to hospital suffering from gastroenteritis whose symptoms – including severe diarrhoea, vomiting and dehydration – I had displayed from the age of two months. My situation was precarious to say the least. Gastroenteritis killed 4.6 million children worldwide in 1980. Only about one in a thousand children succumb to it, while the three most common contributing factors are poor feeding in infancy, consumption of contaminated water and residing in areas of poor sanitation. I was kept in hospital for six months and for some of that time the doctors were unsure that I was going to make it. But I did.

I was back in hospital in 1970, at the age of six, and this time I was suffering from malnutrition and inflammation of the toes. Luckily my father was home on a visit and he brought me in as my mother would never ever bring Patrick or me to the doctor, which is not surprising as she was the source of most, if not all, of our illnesses. I weighed 27lbs, just under two stone. When I was released three weeks later I was four pounds heavier. Looking back on this as an adult I find it a little strange that nobody probed me about my swollen toes. It cannot have been that normal a condition. Patsy never passed any comment at the time either, or so I thought.

By this stage things had settled into a routine at home. Patrick and myself were doing all the housework, and I mean *all* the housework.

Perhaps to keep us housebound we would be dressed in nappies. At around 7 pm every evening she would lay us both down on the floor, side by side, usually in front of our sisters and brothers. Next she would fold up old blankets and pin them around us, sometimes forcing us to wear wet and smelly nappies from the previous night's accident. (I must confess to wetting myself quite frequently, probably thanks to the terror and stress of our home-life.) When this was a novelty she would force us to parade around the house, inviting the others to laugh at us. If there was a needle and thread handy these home-made nappies would be sewn to our tee-shirts to prevent our removing them. Finally the blankets would be covered by a pair of home-made pants, usually a plastic shopping bag, which would be taped to our waist and legs. This went on until we were at least fourteen years old.

A typical morning went (when my father was away in America) as follows: Patrick and I would be woken up at around 6.30 am, well before the others, to start the day's duties. It was his responsibility to prepare the hot breakfast for our sisters and brothers and he did this alone, watched closely by Olive who would stand in the kitchen waiting to strike him should he make any kind of a mistake. Because Patsy was an electrician there was a shed full of equipment out in the back garden, including long tubes of pipe casing, or 'wavin', as we called it, which stung fiercely on impact with our bare skin. Patrick would be sent out to the shed by Olive to choose a length of wire, which she could flick at us, like a jockey goading his horse towards the finishing line, in her guise as the impatient supervisor of our morning's performance. When the breakfast was ready she went to get the others out of bed while I set the table and Patrick lit the fire. As soon everyone was seated, and the food was served up, it was time for Patrick and me to take ourselves outside to the backyard, where we had to polish everyone else's shoes. We did this every morning, in our nappies and bare feet, from January to December; in rain, snow, wind and on the frostiest of days. It was quite a shock to discover that the cold can actually burn. I developed huge blisters on my bloated toes from shivering beside Patrick on those dark, freezing, wet mornings, scrubbing at invisible dirt on shoes we could hardly hold still in our thoroughly numbed hands, while our family sat inside in the light and warmth of the kitchen, enjoying their eggs, bacon and toast, of which we could only inhale the aroma.

Only when all the food had been eaten were we allowed back inside the house to clear the table and wash the dishes. If there were any leftovers: crusts of bread, blobs of butter or egg, the cold, skinny rind of a rasher, she would have me accompany her to the bins where I had to watch the plates being carefully scraped free of any potential nourishment and then, just in case I had any ideas, she would pour a bucket of ash, which had been collected from the fireplace, all over the rubbish. In fact this did not deter us. If we got the chance we just blew the ashes off the food as best as we could and swallowed it down without thinking.

For Patrick, a simple task like cleaning out the grate, which he did every single morning from the age of five, was made absolutely treacherous by Olive's basic rule: there was not to be one speck of dust. But, of course, ash does not need to be dropped by a terrified child in order to contaminate its surroundings; it boldly flies through the air as soon as you try to move it. She stood over him, with the poker in her hand, frequently knocking him about his head and shoulders as he strove to perform the impossible – shovel out the ash from the previous night's fire without allowing *anything* to either fall or fly on to the fireplace or carpet. Once when, in his nervousness, he inevitably dropped some of the blasted ash she became instantly enraged and whacked him so hard on the head that she actually knocked him out.

It is a wonder that neither of us died of pneumonia. During one particularly harsh winter Patrick was frequently shunted outside to tidy the back garden. If he was fully dressed he had to remove all items, including his shoes and stockings, until he was clad in nothing more than his vest and pants, to make sure he was not tempted to escape. When he had finished the job he would turn towards the window where she had placed herself to supervise. There, in answer to his silent request to be let back into the house, she would yell through the glass that the garden was still a mess and to start all over again. To break the monotony of simply watching him trudge around in the rain, or snow, or freezing cold, she would make herself a cup of tea and tap at the window, holding up her mug, and shout at him,

'Would you like some hot tea? Well maybe you can have some in three days time, if you do a good job.'

As a result of these mid-winter barefoot jaunts he ended up with frostbite, but this wasn't even the worst part. Of course she couldn't, or just wouldn't, bring him to the doctors, in case they wanted to know how he ended up in such a state. Instead, a pair of ridiculously over-sized, steel-capped boots that had belonged to my grandfather was crudely fashioned for his ailing feet. The steel caps were removed, leaving them as open as sandals, while Patrick's sore toes were wrapped in bits of old pillow case, for everyone to see, and, not surprisingly, he became the source of much entertainment for his classmates. Because they were several sizes too big for him he could hardly walk in them, looking for all the world like a child trying to imitate a grown-up. He was heartbroken from sheer embarrassment and tearfully begged to be allowed to leave them at home, away from the laughing eyes of the outside world, which, in turn, cheered her up no end. She would be waiting to taunt him herself when he came in from another miserable day at school.

'Well, did your mates like your shoes?'

We were all under orders to field off any enquiries about Patrick's feet by saying that he had an infection. Nothing more.

Our brothers and sisters were afraid of Olive. In 1970 my eldest sister was fourteen years old, Patrick was twelve, and the others were ten, nine, seven and four. When we all walked to and from school, they were ordered to make sure that we didn't drop into our grandparents' house to ask for food, or go to the shops for a loaf of bread. Of course, this is when we were allowed to go to school; more often than not we were locked up in our bedroom until the bruises on our bodies healed. After a while Patrick devised a way of getting us some food, but it required a willing accomplice. It was Michael, the oldest boy after Patrick, who was prepared to take the big risk by helping us. Ironically it only worked when we were under lock and key. Patrick fitted a small shoe into a pair of nylons and dangled it down from our bedroom window until it reached Michael below who would quickly fill the shoe with slices of bread and whatever else he could take unseen from the cupboards. For the more difficult times, that is, when we were able to go to school and therefore were under the obedient and watchful eyes of the others, Michael's solution was to hold as much food as he could in his mouth and drop it just outside the house for us to pick up and shove into our own mouths. No doubt that sounds disgusting, but we were utterly desperate to eat.

Being constantly hungry would drive most men to madness; think of what it does to two young boys. The wrenching stomach pains caused by long-term starvation caused me more tears than any beating she ever gave me, I just couldn't help myself, and the more I cried the more it seemed to spur her on. One of her favourite games was emptying the contents of the fridge and cupboards onto the kitchen table and then ordering an equally hungry Patrick and me to put all the food back into its proper place. Before we began she had us make her a cup of tea so that she could enjoy the show all the more; the show being her two depressed, malnourished sons picking up packs of biscuits, bread, crackers, jam, butter, eggs and whatever else was there, and placing them slowly back on shelves.

There were plenty of times over the years, especially when we were very young, when we would go for up to four days without any kind of nourishment. She even watched to see we didn't drink water from the taps in the bathroom. It was bewildering to wake up hungry and not know when I would get to eat again. Finding the strength to climb out of bed when I was constantly dizzy was a challenge in itself. If she spotted me holding my stomach and crying out of pure hunger she would smile and say something about maybe letting me eat something in a couple of days time, or maybe most definitely I could have something ... next week. Maybe.

We all attended Scoil Mhúire, Tullamore National School, and the best thing about it was that Patrick and I could usually get our hands on some sort of food. As soon as I could I made for the bins at the back of the school where I could nearly always be sure of a couple of slices of bread, complete with bite marks and bits of dirt. When the bell went at lunch-time I trudged home with the others, hoping that perhaps it was my lucky day and she would allow me to eat. And sometimes she did. Sometimes when I sat down at the table and waited in anticipation as plates covered in stew or chips and sausages were handed out to our brothers and sisters, there would be a place set for me – not a normal occurrence – with a knife and fork, which added to my excitement. However I would be given something very different. For me she would take one slice of bread and cut a corner of it, maybe one inch by one inch, place it in the middle of a large plate and tell me to eat it very slowly, using my knife and fork. The ridiculous thing was that I would become so choked up with hot tears of humiliation and hunger that I would almost be unable to eat my 'meal'.

As we got older, Patrick and I learnt to forage for scraps in order to survive. I'm ashamed to say that our poor pet dog, Rebel, went hungry many a night when I was driven to stealing his food. Actually it was Olive who gave me the idea. She would ask Patrick and me if we were hungry and when we'd tentatively – and quite predictably – reply 'yes', she would have us watch her slowly scoop a mountain of food into the dog's bowl and then follow her outside where she put it down in front of the ecstatic animal. We would feel quite desolate over this, and not necessarily because we weren't getting any food, but because it was obvious that our mother loved the dog and hated us.

I also stole from my classmates; some of the kids lived too far from the school to travel home for lunch, so they would bring sandwiches wrapped up in tinfoil or grease-proof paper which, if they didn't look after them, provided me and my brother with sustenance for the day ahead. We always tried to share any food we managed to acquire. Patrick definitely did his best to look out for me and was keenly aware that I was younger than him and altogether too scrawny to defend myself. For instance I lost count of the amount of times I got caught, at school, either retrieving dirty food from the bins or taking a classmate's lunch. Unfortunately, the headmaster must have been unable to imagine what our home life was like. He would call me into his office, not to delve into why on earth a young boy, who came from a reasonably well-off family, was stealing food, of all things, but simply to sternly rebuke me for stealing and follow this, more often than not, by a swift caning on both hands. Better still he would then ring Olive to tell her that I had been thieving food, which meant that a much worse beating awaited me at home, from the woman who would not allow me to eat – my own mother.

When we did find food we were taking a risk in eating it. As soon as we came in from school she would line us both up in front of her in order to smell our breath to make sure we had not eaten anything that day, and woe betide us if she smelt the mouldy bread or whatever we had managed to get our hands on. Our punishment was always a severe beating. One day, when we had not managed to find anything, she accused us both of consuming onions. We both strongly denied this, but received a bashing all the same. I suppose our breath would have been foul, as if we had indeed spent the day chewing raw onion, due to our irregular and sometimes non-existent diet.

One constant supply of food, for which we were eternally grateful, was Bolger's Hotel, which was near the police station. An old guy who kept greyhounds, told Patrick that the staff would hand out a bag of scraps if you presented yourself there at the end of the day and asked them for food for your dog. Either that or the food would be left in bin bags at the back of the hotel. Of course Rebel never got to see any of this. It was better to eat quickly without stopping to look at what we were given. The bag would be a mish-mash of different foods, potatoes, turkey bones and other unidentifiable meats covered with jam and custard, jelly splattered with gravy, with bits of butter squares still in their wrappers, stuck to everything. In the early days, when I was still a toddler, Patrick, at seven or eight years of age, had to scheme how to get the bag of leftovers back into the house, to the room that we were 'held' in.

He remembers today his constant worry over my scrawniness, when you literally could count the bones in my body, and felt that I would surely die of starvation if he didn't do something. He wanted to store food for the future, for the coming weeks when we would be locked up for days without the hope of a crust of bread. Between us we managed to sneak the bag of food through our bedroom window, from the garden below, with the use of twine, and, I would think, a lot of patience on Patrick's part; he was certainly his father's son in terms of his initiative in practical matters. In later years, when we had a bit more freedom, we would run to the quarry and consume the food on the spot. How we never choked on bones I'll never know, we both ate so fast.

# Neighbourhood Watch

*'Mr Doyle was insistent that in other areas his wife is a very good mother and is good to her other five children, but, with Patrick and Kenneth, she insists that they are bad and that they are going to be bad.'*
(Case history, 31 October 1969)

One winter's evening I was walking home, demented with hunger, as usual, and pretty sure that I would not be receiving any food at home for quite a while yet. Suddenly I felt as if I was being physically assaulted by the strong, pungent, smell of heaven that was wafting down the street from the local fish and chip shop. To this day I cannot pass a 'chipper' without remembering the power of those fumes on that particular evening over thirty years ago; it just about sent me sprawling backwards onto the ground. I think that hunger must sharpen the senses because it appeared to me that I could actually hear the crusted coat of the fish harden in the oil. In all honesty 'chipper food', even if Olive had not been starving me, would have been a fantastic novelty for me in itself as neither Patrick nor I would have had many opportunities, at this point, to try it. My pockets were completely empty of coins, but I found it impossible to keep walking and leave that beautiful smell behind. The shop was owned by an Italian family who seemed to know everyone in the town. There were only a couple of customers inside and the friendly wife was pouring salt and vinegar into paper bags that seemed to be crammed with fat, brown chips. How I longed to even just place my tongue against those dark round circles on the bags caused by droplets of grease and vinegar. Before I knew it I had pushed open the door and walked straight up to the counter. She glanced at me in acknowledgement as she took the money from the man beside me. He took his precious bundle and waited for his change. I had no idea what I was going to say until she snapped the cash register shut and looked pointedly at me,

'Yes, please?'

I opened my mouth and heard myself say,

'Have you any scraps for me dog, Rebel?'

She stared at me.

'He's a boxer, see. A big dog and he needs to eat a lot.'

I tried to concentrate on her face, but I couldn't help looking past her to where her husband was dunking more chips and fish and thick sausages covered in batter. It was an incredible sight, as incredible as if I had just discovered Santa's workshop. She muttered something and turned away. Unsure of what she had actually said I continued to wait and drink in the atmosphere.

Perhaps five seconds, or five minutes, passed – I don't know exactly how long – before she was back at the counter and handing me a bag,

'Take this, it isn't much, but it's all that I have.'

I was so grateful, so relieved, so utterly bloody delighted that I hardly said thanks to her. She dismissed me with a curt,

'Don't make this a habit now!'

I almost crashed through the door in my eagerness to eat. Just outside was a phone box, standing empty, I dashed in – like Clark Kent on a deadly serious mission – and plonked myself down, ignoring the unmistakable hint of age-old urine that was to be found in most public phone boxes then, and perhaps still is to this day. I didn't even stop to check if anyone had left any coins in the refund slot; instead I was solely intent on filling my mouth with the bag's contents. I hardly tasted what I was eating; it was more about ridding my belly of the razor sharp pain of starvation. I was in a world of my own, unaware of my surroundings, so that when there was a loud rapping on the window, just above my head, I shrieked in absolute fright and confusion thinking that Olive must have followed me and now I was caught like a rat in a trap. It was a heady relief to see the woman from the chipper peering in, looking as confused as I felt. I pushed open the door a little.

'I thought you said this was for your dog.'

'Ye-es it was, I mean, is. It's just that I was a bit hungry so I was just having a bite before bringing it home. To Rebel.'

She shook her head quickly and because I didn't know what else to say I said I was sorry. Pulling open the door as far as it would go she beckoned to me,

'Come inside. Keep that for Rebel, I will give you something for yourself. Yes?'

And so she did. She made me sit down and presented me with a meal fit for Gay Byrne or the Pope. I presume I was thrashed when I got home, but I don't remember. What I do remember, however, are the chips, covered in rivulets of tomato sauce, and the battered cod, shimmering under the puddles of vinegar that accumulated in its ridges, with two slices of thickly buttered white bread that was my unexpected prize that evening.

When I was nine years old I was sent to Temple Street Children's Hospital, suffering from severe abdominal pains. My 'worried' mother explained that, for some reason she couldn't fathom, I was unable to keep my food down. After a lot of tests it was agreed that I might be suffering from Celiac Sprue, a disorder of the small intestine. Certainly my symptoms seemed appropriate: chronic diarrhoea, stomach cramps, lacking ability to put on weight and constant fatigue bordering on depression, which might lead to disturbing behaviour at school. Even to my nine-year-old mind my symptoms screamed another possible diagnosis: I was being starved at home and therefore so hungry, all of the time, that I was eating anything at all, from the unwashed, not fully-grown vegetables I pulled out of the neighbours' back gardens, including raw potatoes, to Rebel's dog food. Bin day had become a favourite for me and Patrick, as it was the day on which it seemed to us that the streets were positively lined with gold, or, in other words, lined with filthy bins from which we would pluck stale, normally inedible foodstuffs. We would scurry like mice from bin to bin, as if running a relay race. All we lacked was a baton; he would take one and I would dart past him to take the other. Mere seconds were all that was needed to divulge a bin's contents, and as we became more practised, no time was wasted. I suppose it was naive of us to assume that this went completely unnoticed by the locals.

When he was in primary school, Patrick confided in a friend in his class about not being allowed to eat at home. This obviously made an impression on the young boy because he told his mother about Patrick's predicament. A hobby among some of the schoolboys at the time was lamping pigeons of an evening, so from then on, each morning before school Patrick was presented with a whole cooked pigeon plus a sandwich, courtesy of his classmate's mother. She even went as far as writing his name on a note, and sticking it onto the wrapped food, so that there would be no doubt that the food was really his. The same thing happened when Patrick confided in another young friend about his being starved at home. When Patrick would pass the boy's house on his way to school, the mother would be hiding in her doorway, waiting for him, and would call out,

'Young Doyle, come in here and have some breakfast.'

This went on for quite a while, until one awful morning when, in the middle of his secret meal, Patrick realised the jig was up. Olive was outside shouting for him. Patrick froze, petrified at the sound of his mother's voice, while his school-friend's kind-hearted mother bustled out to confront her. There was no point in denying anything, but Olive was certainly not going to apologise for her actions.

'If you fed your children like a normal person then they wouldn't be eating out of bins!'

Olive ignored the other woman and continued shouting for Patrick to show himself.

'I'm telling you now I'm going to report you to the SPCC. It's an absolute disgrace!'

Patrick was dragged back to our house and grilled on every word that his friend's mother had ever said to him. When the interrogation was over she stripped him bare and put him in one of her home-made nappies, this one concocted from half a woollen blanket that was folded over and sewn together, which she wrapped in a plastic bin liner. And then he was beaten senseless and locked up until the bruises faded.

He was even fed, on the quiet, by the nuns at school. Now this did not mean that he was a favourite, or doted upon in any way. In fact the nuns came down hard on him thanks solely to Olive. Anyone who has ever attended a convent school knows that nuns are fairly rigid when it comes to rules and regulations – and, in particular, punctuality. Our mother certainly knew that, which was why she took great enjoyment in sweeping out the others to be on time while holding on to Patrick. Scoil Mhúire is a ten-minute walk from the house and pupils had to be at their desks by 9 o'clock, on the dot. So the others would be waved off at a quarter to nine, to reach the school with five minutes to spare while Patrick was prevented from leaving until the clock struck five minutes after the hour, thus making him a terrifying fifteen minutes late. When his mother was asked to send in a note to explain his constant tardiness she penned one claiming that she always sent Patrick out to school with his brothers and sisters, but that she couldn't do anything with him anymore and he had probably stopped to shoplift on the way. And so forth. It was really quite clever of her, not only would Patrick be blamed for his inability to be in school on time but now, thanks to his mother, everyone took him for a thief, and more importantly, a liar – just in case he ever told stories about his dreadful home life.

One nun would have one of our sisters brought out of her class, to the office, so that she could witness her brother being caned while the head nun, who seemed to dislike him as much as the other nuns, would summon Patrick to her office every morning to feed him with bread, cheese and mugs of cocoa.

The doctors kept me in for a couple of weeks and put me on a gluten-free diet, the only treatment for this condition. I didn't ever want to leave; friendly nurses, three meals a day, and I was miles away from the claustrophobic and poisonous atmosphere of the house in Tullamore. It was blissful to be the object of good attention as opposed to being the focus of my mother's rage and maliciousness. But of course I had to return home some time, and in fact things were not too bad – for a couple of days at any rate. My mother taunted me, calling me 'Celli', after Celiac Sprue. She had nicknames for most of her children and this was to be mine, as long as my father wasn't around, until I finally left her house in my sixteenth year.

A few days later a district social worker came to visit me at home, bringing a selection of gluten-free products, breads and biscuits for me. My mother had been told that I had to have a gluten-free diet for the rest of my life or I would end up back in hospital every so often with the same complaint. As soon as the social worker left Olive called me into the kitchen and ordered me to break up the bread and biscuits into little pieces. From there she brought me out into the back garden where I had to fling everything up high onto the roof so that the birds could have their pickings without any danger of my grabbing something.

# 'A Woman's Work'

*'It appears that Patrick has to do all the housework ... While his father is away from home she will give him nothing to eat ...'*
(Case History, 31 October 1969)

A woman's work is never done. That's the old saying and if it is referring to the hours of labour required to keep a house clean then I completely agree. It wasn't just that Patrick and I had to cook meals, set tables, clear tables, wash dishes, dry dishes, make all the beds, wash floors, dust the many ornaments and intricate cuts of Waterford glass crystal, light the fire and clean out the fire. Doing all of those basic chores would have been relatively little to contend with; it was the other extras that Olive had us perform that I had a problem with. For instance Patsy had bought her a very fine vacuum cleaner, but it was only used in front of him during his visits home. The rest of the time I had to hand pick the dirt out of the carpets, which meant crawling around the relevant rooms, on my hands and knees, in the nude, and if I missed a speck of something I would be punished; that is, beaten severely, and ordered to start all over again. The whole process literally took hours and hours, and was back-breaking, especially if I had not eaten in a few days and was having trouble focusing on minute particles of dust. Remember that ours was a full house, with at least eight children at any given time.

Equally demanding, in the physical sense, was her novel way of drying clothes. Of course we would have washed the blankets, sheets, towels and patchwork quilts in the first place. Frequently she would roughly wake us up at maybe three or four o'clock in the morning to begin the day's laundry. I remember our neighbours telling her she was great for having her big washing done so early in the morning, not realising that she would have had her two weakling slaves hard at it while everyone else was still fast asleep. Seating herself comfortably on a chair, she issued her instructions. We would lug a mountain of bed linen and towels into the bathroom where we had to hand wash them in the bath, using only ice cold water. I don't fully understand why she always had us use cold water, perhaps it was simply to make our tasks even more difficult. And it was an immensely difficult task, especially for an underweight five year old; the weight of the towels and sheets – once they had been submerged in water – was torturous. When she decided that each item was clean enough we had to wring them out, handful by handful, which required some amount of strength, until our hands were purple from the strain and the cold. More often than not she decided that we were doing it all wrong and would fling us both into the freezing water, on top of the washing. I had long, skinny fingers that she would bend backwards, telling me I wasn't working hard enough. If I started to cry, no matter how hard I tried not to, it was like waving a red flag at a demented bull, and encouraged her to hurt me even more.

She had a problem about putting dripping wet clothes straight on to the line, preferring to shed the excess water first. So, on windy mornings, she had us stand outside in the back garden holding up, as high as we could manage, heavy, drenched sheets and towels for a couple of hours until she decided they were fit to be pegged to the line. I must have looked like some sort of dwarf, scraggy scarecrow, or else a giant garden gnome. The aching of my childish arms – in fact the ache would spread across both my shoulders, turning to creep on up to my neck, before doubling back down my spine, vertebrae by vertebrae, and eventually charging down my legs – stayed with me for days afterwards.

Three times a week Patrick had to scrub the lino in the hall; the measurement of which was approximately nineteen by thirty feet. At least he was allowed to use a nail brush, in the place of his finger nails, although he had to make do with one bucket of cold water. The whole process took hours, however, as he had to clean it *her* way, which meant dividing the job up into squares, of maybe twelve by twelve inches, and spending up to fifteen minutes on each square. Her inevitable harassment of him would only commence half-way through the job, just when he felt he was getting somewhere and the end was in sight. Bending over to peer closely at the well-scrubbed floor, while he continued feverishly working away, she would 'find' a dirty spot and explode. Before he knew it the mucky contents of the bucket were either poured over him or else kicked over onto the area he had just spent hours cleaning. If it was the latter treatment he was made kneel in the dirty, cold puddle and told to start again. If it was a particularly bad day she would drag him through the water, all the while beating him with that day's weapon of choice. He remembers her literally dancing with rage and screaming blue murder, before getting a chair for herself and an alarm clock, shouting, as she sat down, that he had such and such *seconds* to get the floor dried – an impossible task, while in truth, she knew it and he knew it, it was mere foreplay before she beat the crap out of him again.

The consequences of her hatred were a lot more complicated than simply beating or depriving us of food. It seemed that she also wanted, or needed, us to experience sheer humiliation. Sometimes, especially during school holidays, she allowed us to look out the landing window so that we could see our friends playing, having the time of their lives, or fishing at the lake. Our longing to be outside was obviously transparent, and she would get a kick out of tormenting us.

'Wouldn't you like to be out playing with your friends?'

Undecided whether it was worse to answer 'yes' or 'no', we would stare warily at her as she smiled and told us,

'Aw, what a pity you can't, you've too much housework to do.'

I was about six years of age when my little sister was born and it was my job to wash her nappies in the toilet. We had a washing machine and we could certainly afford rubber gloves and fancy cleaning agents, yet I had to wash the numerous soiled nappies using just my bare hands – to pick off every bit of shit – and cold toilet water. Sometimes, when I was feeling particularly weak, I would end up adding my own vomit to the excrement as the smell was overwhelming. When I was finished I had to bring my work to be inspected and if she spotted anything it meant another beating and back to the toilet to finish the job properly. I suppose I should be a little bit grateful, considering this particular task – albeit temporarily – killed my appetite stone dead.

Meanwhile one of Patrick's daily tasks was to clean the toilet, with his bare hands and finger nails. He was required to spend an hour doing this. Olive liked to write out a list of our duties accompanied by the length of time that she decided each job should take us. As was the norm Olive would stand behind him watching him rub the toilet bowl with the palms of his hands, while hers contained a tube of wavin, as chosen by him, which she would liberally apply to his upper body.

When he was very young Patrick remembers being used as a sort of dressing table. He had to kneel down in front of my mother, who was seated in a comfortable chair, and hold up a mirror so that she could carefully check her face for spots, his little arms ached after thirty minutes, but he dared not complain, so focused was she on finding imperfections in her reflection.

I would imagine that Patrick and I learned about such things as periods and bras at a much earlier stage than most girls. For some reason Olive had me and Patrick strap her flabby body into her bra and corset every morning. Perhaps she was a subscriber to that old adage about keeping your enemies closer to you than your friends. Well, she had no friends and she certainly seemed to view me and my brother as her sworn enemies. We were also charged with finding and plucking any grey hairs from her head. If we tried to tell her that she had none she would scream that we must be fucking blind as well as stupid. Another favourite pastime was to have us scratch her fat back for anything up to an hour at a time. For this she would remove her top and sit in her bra, as regal and proud as a queen on her throne, while we, her minions, scratched and scratched. We were also ordered to locate and squeeze any blackheads that she had. Very often we would pretend to find some and would obediently go through the motions of squeezing as she asked us about the colour and texture of our find. Even at my young age this troubled me. As did her searching both our heads, in turn, for grey hairs. She would make us, one at a time, place our heads face down, right into her crotch, while she picked through every strand of hair.

When we were very young she would hold our faces right next to hers while she carefully searched, and physically dug into our young skin, pulling it up and down with her nails, looking for any lurking blackheads. Sometimes she actually drew blood. It really, really hurt. I have yet to meet a child under the age of ten who is plagued by either blackheads or grey hairs.

Our schooling in the traditionally secretive subject of

menstruation came about when she had us add the washing of her sanitary towels to our list of household duties. She was very proud of the fact that she didn't buy her sanitary towels; instead she made them out of old towels. When her cycle was over we were handed the bucket of her bloodied bits of material and, as with the nappies, we were only allowed to use our bare hands and cold water, while she waited impatiently to view our handiwork. No prize for guessing what happened if they were not cleaned to her satisfaction. It was a nine-month long relief for us when Patsy had her knocked up after one of his annual visits home. Torturing us was a full-time job for her and she literally refused to take a break away from us. Above all was her constant fear that she might inadvertently, through her own negligence, present us with the opportunity to grab some food from her kitchen. The poor woman felt she couldn't take her eye off us, even for the few minutes that she needed to sit on the toilet. After all, she was only human, and nature called for her just as it did for everyone else. However, she soon solved the problem in her usual clever way by rigidly ignoring the two pristine (thanks to me and Patrick) bathrooms. Instead one of us would be sent out to the garden shed to fetch the bucket into which she would pee or shit – and we would be made to stand in front of her and watch – thereby robbing us of even the briefest chance to grab a slice of unbuttered bread. Naturally, when she was finished, either Patrick or I would be told to take the bucket outside, relieve it of its contents and give it a thorough clean. Later on she decided to substitute the old worn bucket for the relative luxury of sitting down on the toilet; certainly the bucket would never have taken her weight. By this stage whichever one of us she had recently beaten would be tied to her arm or leg; such was her fear that we might escape and our bruises be seen by our neighbours.

Few children can have known their mothers as well as we knew ours, inside and out.

# Robber Doyles

*'The situation at home has continued and he has been aware of it, at least, since 1965 when the ISPCC were called in and it is only now that he is beginning to do something about it. I feel it would be important to keep a close contact with Mr Doyle and the two boys at this point.'*

(Case History, 31 October 1969)

What's the old radio advertisement? 'Dunnes Stores better value beats them all'? This was certainly true in our house, especially after Patrick and I were made responsible for most of the shopping. Only it wasn't so much shopping as out and out stealing. It was as if this was the reason she gave birth to us. I don't know when she came up with the idea but, with hindsight, Olive put into action a highly effective, and profitable, system. We became very adept at thieving, both Patrick and me. We stole food, stole money to buy food and, most importantly, stole for Olive to stop her beating us for a couple of days. To our relief and immense joy we discovered that turning up with stolen bounty for our mother made her laugh out loud and dance with joy straight to the kitchen where she would pop a couple of slices of bread into the toaster and put the kettle on for a cup of tea, for the bashful, dutiful thief. It was like the film *Oliver Twist*; I have never read the book by Charles Dickens. We were two hungry 'Artful Dodgers' while she was a nasty combination of Fagin and Bill Sykes. I can't remember how it all started, but I do remember squirming in embarrassment on learning that our local nickname was the 'Robber Doyles'. My particular forte was the tens of parked cars that were strewn across the town on any given day, though some days were better than others. For instance Sundays, the national day of rest, were probably my busiest. Once the church bell started summoning the faithful to its morning masses – 8.30, 9.30, 10.30, 11.30 and 12.30 – I went to work. Our brothers and sisters went to the children's mass at 10 am, but neither Patrick nor I had to attend it. We had far more ignoble matters to devote ourselves to.

Olive had no qualms about letting us out of the house, providing we brought something back and didn't return in a squad car. The first provision was much easier to accomplish than the second, since our reputation overtook us in due course. I take no pride today in admitting that it is probably thanks to the likes of me that people are so careful about locking their cars now. Unfortunately, for my neighbours, the trustworthy nature common to inhabitants of small towns in the 1960s and 70s meant that I didn't have to waste any time in picking locks. All I had to do was open the door and take anything that might feed me or keep Olive relatively happy – on a strictly temporary basis, of course. I usually had my choice of newspapers. She asked me specifically to bring back *The Sunday World*, *News of the World* and *The People*. Most of the time I was lucky; these three very same papers would be sitting, one on top of the other, in someone's passenger seat. If it was the case that I only managed to get two out of three and, say for example, the *Farmer's Journal*, then I simply took myself off the local newsagents and politely explained how I bought the wrong paper for the mother. It was immediately exchanged for the right paper.

For bonus points I would head back in the direction of the church, to the small sweet and toy shop next door, and there I would wait until the mass was over and the – in those days enormous – congregation filed out and into the little confectionery store. Perhaps all the kids had been promised sweets if they stayed quiet during mass. When the place was heaving with customers I'd slide into the middle of the crowd and basically help myself to whatever I could. The free newspapers were a given, to get fed that day I'd need to bring something else home, even if it was only a cheap toy that would be automatically given to my baby brother. It was the difference between me getting a couple of slices of bread and absolutely nothing.

She would send us back out on Sunday afternoons to find what we could. This time we would enter the church, but not to pray, nor ask forgiveness for missing mass. We had the place to ourselves and could take our time, carefully checking under every row of seats for any coins that had been dropped in the rush to fill the priest's plate. It usually provided us with a couple of big coins, like fifty pence pieces. On leaner days we'd actually break into the steel candle box for heavy handfuls of dirty copper. Thanks to the innocence of the time it was ridiculously easy to open the container; nobody expected anyone to have the gall, or indeed, the desperation, to rob the candle coffer, of all things. We narrowly escaped getting caught one Sunday. Sometimes when the attendance at mass was big a lot of people were forced to hear the sermon outside the church door. To make sure the church didn't lose out in any way – from an economic point of view – a collection box was placed out in the churchyard, on a small table, for these busy times. Naturally, as soon as the coast was clear, I went for it. To my consternation I found that the box was chained to the table obliging me to take both of them with me. I carried them around to the back of the church where I thought I'd be free to open the box in peace. But, as they say, God works in mysterious ways. Just as I was attacking the box a parishioner happened upon me. I don't know who gave who the bigger shock. He yelled out in disbelief and I took off, with the table leg banging against my own. There was no way he was going to catch me. I threw the table and box into a big bush on the church grounds, not slowing down until I reached the other side of town.

Aside from mass the other good thing about Sundays were the GAA matches, which took place rain or shine. When necessary – if our superficial ransacking of the church had not turned up anything decent – Patrick and I would make our way to the local club, or, to be more accurate, the local club's small dressing room. Roars of approval or disapproval, depending on who supported who, filled the air as Patrick helped me through the tiny square window, all the while keeping a constant eye out for wandering fans or team-mates. We never thought to check how long the game had been on; therefore every second was utterly precious. The room smelled of old sweat and cheap aftershave and contained the belongings of all the players who were out strutting their stuff on the field. It didn't take me long to rifle through the twenty odd pairs of trousers and bags, made easier by the fact that I only wanted money, nothing else. With the door to the changing room locked during play and the window much too small for your average-sized eight year old the players didn't go to any great lengths to hide away their wallets. I moved from one pile of clothes to the next, coldly emptying the wallets, not even bothering with coins, throwing them down and within minutes Patrick was pulling me back out into the fresh air. No one was safe from the Robber Doyles.

The Tullamore branch of Dunnes Stores, which sat beside the police station, was a terrifically busy one when we were kids. Selling everything from food to toys to household products people travelled from miles around to do their weekly shopping. The shop security was provided by plainclothes store detectives. In the good old days, before my face became far too familiar with the staff, the shop was a dream. For one thing the farmers and their families who had driven many miles to do their shopping could, after paying for their purchases, leave their heavy bags sitting in a trolley while they went off to buy something up the street, or go in for a jar. It was a convenient gesture, on behalf on Dunnes, which made their customers' lives a lot easier, and, more importantly, mine too. All that was required was for me to look utterly law-abiding as I strode to the relevant bay and seized hold of a full trolley, neither looking left or right, nor hinting that anything remotely out of the ordinary was taking place. I was merely an obedient son sent to collect the family shopping for my parents, loyal Dunnes customers, who were just finishing their second pot of tea in the local café. In fact there *was* a lot of truth in my performance; I was being nothing less than an obedient son. The trick was to keep going no matter what. Once I had commandeered the trolley I pushed my way to the exit, being careful not to go too fast, because unnecessary speed might suggest that all was not as it appeared. It never occurred to me to pilfer something from the bags on the walk home, before I presented it to Olive. For one thing I was in a rush to surprise her and see her smile at me, and for another I suppose I much preferred that she, my mother, give me the toast and tea irrespective of anything superior in taste and variety that was in the trolley.

School friends became my innocent accomplices when the going got tough. Inevitably it was only a matter of time – and trolleys – before my entrance was connected with irate customers waving their receipts and generally causing havoc for busy staff over their missing shopping. At some point I could no longer walk over the threshold of the shop so I resorted to 'Plan B'. I stood outside the building and waited patiently until

I spotted a boy I knew. Making sure I saw him before he saw me I would pretend to be crying as he greeted me.

'Hey Ken, what's up with you?'

Nobody ever remarks on the kindness of school boys.

'Oh, … sniff …, hi, … sniff.'

'Well, what's wrong?'

'My mother … sniff … sent me to get the messages. Only … sniff … when I had paid for everything, the stupid manager threw me out of the shop. … Sniff, sniff … He wouldn't … sniff … even let me take my mother's stuff … sniff. She's going to kill me if I go home without it. Sniff … I don't know what I'm going to do …'

Invariably my friend would reply,

'Ach don't worry Ken. Stop crying, I'll get them for you. Just show me where they are.'

Quite a lot of my classmates helped me out in this way, never for one moment suspicious of the fact that they were stealing some poor bugger's shopping. I can honestly say that I never experienced the slightest twinge of guilt for any of this. Stealing meant something much bigger than breaking grown-up rules or committing a sin, it meant being made food by a – briefly – smiling, seemingly loving mother. I would have done anything for that. Sometimes she sent me to Dunnes with specific requests for their extra large Sun Haze tights and towels, both of which were a favourite with her. These were ridiculously easy to procure, especially before I became infamous. She always gave me the money with the instructions to bring it straight back to her. Not the change, you understand, but the actual note she gave me. This went for all kinds of purchases, big and small. This was a clever way of covering herself should we get caught robbing. She could point out quite truthfully that she gave us the money and therefore had no earthly idea why we would shame her by resorting to shoplifting.

Patrick was given the slightly scary job of 'collecting' her full trolley from Dunnes. She would fill a trolley and then just push it aside, perhaps telling someone she had forgotten her purse or else successfully hiding it away in a different department. As soon as she got home Patrick would be told where to find it and off he went to retrieve the unpaid goods and bring them safely back to her. If she wanted something fancier than food, like clothes or footwear, she would 'shop' for what she wanted, in her size and colour, but instead of paying for the items, she would hide them somewhere about the premises and Patrick would have to go and 'collect' them.

One day she made out a long shopping list and went off to Dunnes Stores. About an hour later I was a little surprised to see her back at the house with her shopping trolley full of bags; in other words she had paid for it all. However she wasn't done yet. Calling me to her she presented me with both her till receipt and her original shopping list and told me to bring the trolley back to Dunnes and fill it up a second time, only this time I was to dispense with the plastic bags. In other words, I was to leave without paying for this second shopping spree. To this day I cannot work out how I got away with it. Picture it; a skinny kid with a long list, dangling from his hand, pushing a trolley he can barely see over, painstakingly threading his way up and down the aisles, tense with concentration, and then, when the trolley is filled to the brim, he, barely owning the strength to move the heavy load, making his way very carefully, via a relatively long and unsure walk, to the exit door. It was nothing short of a miracle. Maybe God was on Olive's side?

It was something that puzzled us. Patsy's envelopes from America were always regular and generous. She had plenty of money, probably more than any of our neighbours, yet she really got a tremendous kick out of acquiring things without exchanging money for them. Even milk. The milkman lived up near the hospital and it was he who delivered just about everybody's milk in the town. Before he began his rounds his packed lorry sat outside his house while he had his breakfast. Early in the morning Olive would give me money for six cartons of milk, telling me to bring back the coins in full. It was all too easy. I would dart up to the truck and grab a case of milk. A case held eight cartons so this meant I could knock back two pints before bringing the requested six back for the others' Cornflakes and Rice Crispies. This poor milkman was subjected to my badness a second time after I came up with an ingenious plan one particularly desperate evening. I was only about eight or nine years old at the time, and urgently looking about the deserted town for something to take back to Olive. It had been a quiet day all round and I had no intention of being beaten for returning home empty-handed. Plus I was cold and hungry and, for once, unable to accept the idea of not eating until some time later, the following day. I was filled with a righteous indignation at the unlocked cars that proved empty as far as food, money or treasure went. This had never happened before in my short career of amateur thievery. Unfortunately, by the time I had realised the futility of searching through numerous parked cars, it was well after 6 pm, so my usual mecca, Dunnes Stores, was closed, as were the rest of the shops. A bubble of familiar fear began to grow within my chest. Surely there must be something I could take. Time was running out as I hadn't been home since morning, otherwise I might have hung about until the pubs closed, hoping to bump into one of my 'usuals'. There was one farmer who, under the influence, could comfortably be codded out of a few pounds with the promise of delivery of an imaginary sheep. He never seemed to find it strange that he was doing business, at ungodly hours, with a nine year old, or if he did, he never remarked upon it. I would simply describe the attractiveness of said ewe, or ram, and assure him that he was getting, by far, my best price. By this particular evening I possibly owed him an imaginary flock, but thankfully he never remembered one encounter from the next. After a few attempts to bargain me down we would agree on a price, to be paid immediately, shake hands like the two gentlemen we genuinely believed ourselves to be, before heading off happily in opposite directions. However he was nowhere to be seen on this particular night.

I continued to walk the quiet streets, not prepared to admit defeat until it was 100 per cent impossible to do anything else. And then it hit me. As I looked from house to house I spied empty milk bottles in the porches. Some houses had as many as seven empties waiting to be exchanged for full bottles the next morning. That man must make a fortune, I thought, as the hum of an idea began to whirr in my head. At first I wondered if there was a way I could sell milk, stolen, naturally, from the milkman's truck, to the townspeople. Taking the time to consider the possibilities I was forced to finally admit that the location was all wrong. The milkman's truck was about a mile away from where I was and in truth I would only be able to carry maybe six bottles at a time. Therefore the profit would not be worth the time and energy required to make it. (It is amazing the clarity of one's mind, despite youth, when you have to literally earn every single mouthful.) Then, as I stared dolefully at the silent group of empties outside one well-lit house it came to me. An idea whose perfection and beauty was borne from its abject simplicity. What if I cut out the delivering of the milk and skipped, instead, to the taking of the payment?

By the time the plan was fully realised I was standing outside a grand-sized house that was of no use to me since it housed another farmer who walked through the town every day with his own milk vending machines, his ten or so cows. I kept going until I reached the front door of his neighbour. A kindly-looking woman answered my tentative knock.

'Hello Missus, the milkman is sick so he can't collect his money tomorrow. I'm helping him by collecting it tonight.'

'Oh dear, I hope it's not too serious. Well, isn't he lucky that he has a good little boy like yourself to be helping him out like this?'

'Erm, yes thanks. Do you know how much milk you had delivered this week?'

'Now, let me see. I had two on Monday, three on Tuesday and Wednesday ... yes that would make it twelve pints altogether. So I owe you five, ten, fifteen … yes, sixty pence, and sure here's a little something for yourself for being such a good helper.'

I worked my way up her side of the road until I made the princely sum of £5. It was enough for some food and a jig from my mother. On the other hand it would be a long, long time before I felt brave enough to set foot on that street again.

Olive had a passion for Waterford Crystal. Luckily for me it was easy to get. Kilroy's was a popular local shop that sold all sorts of pricey kitchenware like fancy delph, expensive pots and pans and lovely, lovely pieces, in various sizes and forms, of the famous crystal. She had expensive tastes, my mother. Only the best for her. As I said it was very easy to acquire, as long as I didn't mind not having a bag to hide what I was carrying. I didn't. The crystal was always part of the window display so all I had to do was wait for the inevitable opportunity to calmly walk in, climb nimbly into the window, which was conveniently positioned right beside the front door, and grab a piece. Sometimes the shop assistant might have to go to the back of the shop to fetch something for a customer or they might be wholly engaged in a serious conversation about the capabilities of a particular saucepan. I'm inclined to think it was probably a common enough sight; that is, me running grim-faced through town, homewards, with a crystal clock or sugar bowl clutched against my skinny chest. I built up quite a collection for her: jugs, decanters, bowls, vases and an ice bucket. She had so many pieces of the stuff she had Patsy build her a display cabinet for it, which was put in the front room, the room where visitors were seated, should there be any. Ironically, the most frequent visitors to the house were the Gardaí, who were bringing either me or Patrick home after we'd been caught robbing, yet again. I was much too young to appreciate the irony of those men of the law sipping tea from a set of china that was stamped with 18 ct gold, which Patrick had nicked from a car parked in Market Square. The silver buttons against their dark navy uniforms winked in the reflection of the display cabinet that was filled to the brim with stolen Waterford Crystal.

I don't think anybody would have described Olive as a romantic woman, but my, how she loved her red roses. Only they weren't exactly her red roses. Our front garden was like a showpiece, or maybe it would be more accurate to say that it served to highlight the best of what our neighbours' gardens had to offer. Patrick was sent out at night, with a shovel, a plastic bag and pair of rubber gloves, to retrieve the rose bushes that Olive had spotted in someone else's garden, for her own personal collection. She also had a fancy for garden gnomes, that is, other people's garden gnomes. If the gnomes that suddenly found themselves sitting in our garden could talk they'd have a shocking story to tell.

Keeping my mother happy became something of an obsession for me and Patrick. When she was especially pleased it meant two definite days without beatings. The reward never stretched to three days so we were kept busy thieving. If I could have focused my initiative on my school work instead I think I'd be a richer man today. There was another shop, Gleeson's, which sold quality curtains and furnishings. For some reason I found myself there one day. The sales woman opened a press behind the counter and I spied a large box with a woman's name on it. Let's say that the name was Mary Kennedy. Without even thinking about it, such was my adeptness for seizing the slightest of occasions to make money, I presented myself at the cash desk and told the woman that I had been sent to pick up a package for Mrs Kennedy, who was sick and couldn't come to get it herself.

'OK, pet, just let me see if her order is in yet.'

It was, of course.

I ran to the quarry where I could safely tear open the box and inspect its contents. I don't know what I expected to find, but my mind was racing with images of a tottering stack of buttered bread, or another fish 'n' chips feast. Inexplicably, I was crushed to find the box full of nothing else but curtains. After staring at them for some minutes I thought I might as well bring them back to Olive. Well my disappointment turned to heady delight when I saw her ecstatic reaction. It turned out they were only the best type of curtains that money could buy and there was one, perfectly measured out, for every window of our house. I remember I got a small dollop of raspberry jam that day, on top of the buttered toast.

The strange thing was that it really didn't seem to matter to Olive the size or value of what we brought home to her. I had certainly done well with the curtains, but it seemed to Patrick and me that she was just as pleased with a bit of stolen bacon. Perhaps Dunnes Stores only true – albeit minor – competitor was the little store/garage across the Clara Bridge. It was also a particular favourite of mine because its very size and popularity made it extremely easy to take something. For folks heading back 'to the country' – basically all land that was more than a mile away from Tullamore – the shop was the last stop for petrol and essentials such as milk and the daily newspaper. There was always a pallet of milk outside, but it was left in full view of the family who ran the business. Therefore I had to wait until it got dark, which I patiently did, usually in the stomach of a large piece of discarded farm machinery that sat nearby almost covered by its coat of dandelion fluff and overgrown weeds. There is an awful lot of waiting in robbing. When it was dark and the shop was filled with workers preparing for the drive home I would sneak in beside someone, making it appear, to the casual observer, that I was their offspring. Then I would help myself. The meat was stored in a big freezer sitting inside the door and, because I hadn't got a bag, frozen packs of temporarily iced bacon had to be reluctantly pushed down the front of my trousers. This, as you can imagine, produced a thoroughly unpleasant sensation, only surpassed by the pain which accompanied the removal of the packs – that is the stripping of the vacuumed plastic away from my cowering, terrified penis. Once my cargo was in its stinging place I could grab some milk, under the cover of darkness, as I exited the shop. Presenting Olive with the money she had given me to 'get' milk, the milk itself and then the unexpected meat won me, at the very least, that evening free from a beating.

# 'Cheese Please!'

*'My impression from meeting Mr Doyle and Kenneth was of a depressed boy whose physical and mental health ... is seriously at risk in his present environment. The onset of this child's battering, based on Mr Doyle's allegations, would appear to have commenced when he was approximately eighteen months old. Should only one twentieth of the allegations of Mr Doyle about the abuse of Kenneth by his mother be true, he would still be seriously at risk.'*

(Moore Abbey Psychological Service, 30 January 1976)

We were beaten nearly every single day. Only God knows why. I'm not even sure if Olive herself knows the reason why she hated us so. Patrick thinks that it might have been something to do with the fact that he and I physically resembled Patsy more than the others. And their marriage certainly did not appear to be a happy one when we were growing up. Despite that, whether it was merely to keep the peace, she often successfully enlisted Patsy in thrashing us. She was careful to curtail her own violence towards us during his visits, but that's not to say we were left in peace. His beatings, however, were nowhere near as horrific as hers. Her behaviour, at times, was downright vindictive, almost as if we were involved in some kind of secretive, torturous game; 'we' being me, Patrick and Olive. For instance when Patsy was home from America she would have the entire family seated around the table and serve us up a big dinner. Our portions would be the same as our brothers and sisters; only, unlike our siblings, Patrick and I knew we had mere seconds to eat as much as we could before we were signalled, with rapid blinking from our mother, to stop eating, lay down our knife and fork, slide our plate away from us and stare blankly ahead. Our father would immediately ask what was wrong, to which we had no good answer. It thoroughly annoyed him to see any food going to waste. Then she would feign a fretful hurt over our disrespectful behaviour.

'Look at how they insult me Pat, refusing to eat the dinner I've spent hours making. These two will be the death of me!'

'Eat your dinners.'

All we could do was hang our heads in silent misery. If we took another bite she would make us pay for it later, when he was at the pub, and if we didn't ...

Patsy stared angrily at us both in turn.

'I *said*, eat your bloody dinners.'

I willed him to understand what was going on; that despite our ferocious hunger, we weren't eating our dinner because she had told us we weren't to, on her signal. Couldn't he see that he was just a pawn in her harassment of us? When we were much younger, before he left to go away for work, and he could see that we weren't being fed he would sneak us food, warning us – unnecessarily – not to tell Olive. Our cooperation with her blinking eyes had been worked out before our father's arrival from America. On the day his plane landed in Ireland for his month-long, Christmas visit, she cornered us together, explaining that if we didn't want to be beaten to death in January, (which we naturally believed to be a definite possibility) we were both to refuse to eat in front of him.

Unable to contain her mounting excitement as Patsy's voice increased in volume and rage she began to shout breathlessly,

'Kill them Pat, kill them! They're no good. You've no idea what they put me through when you're away.'

Predictably he would give her what she so badly wanted, indeed what she seemed to yearn for; as other people yearn for the more typical vices of alcohol, nicotine or sugar. We were both told to go to our room and wait for him while he finished his dinner. Her look was one of smug ecstasy as we stood up and left the table. In our room I would pray, in vain, asking God to take me quickly before my father's heavy footsteps were heard on the stairs. Neither Patrick nor I made the slightest attempt at a conversation. What was there to say? A few short minutes later and a mute Patsy came in, his belt already off and in his hand. He beat us for maybe five, maybe ten minutes – although you can be sure about one thing, it always seemed longer to us. We were then sent to bed hungry, as an added punishment for upsetting our poor, over-worked mother, which of course, whether Patsy knew this or not, was a normal day's work for us. To be honest the belt didn't hurt that much, or at least not in comparison to my mother's choice of weaponry. I mean, if Patrick and I were ever given a choice of what we'd like to be beaten with – which never happened – we would automatically choose the belt without having to debate the subject.

Olive would sing to us, but not in the normal way a mother sings to soothe a child. No, she would sing only to taunt and terrify us. Aside from setting us up for Patsy, the four weeks of his Christmas holiday were, more or less, peaceful; or, at least there was a welcome respite in the routine of daily beatings. The last week before his return to work was always a tense one. It was as if we could actually hear the minutes tick away, with frequent hushed reminders from Olive about what she was going to do to us as soon as Patsy closed the door behind him. That she was looking forward to his leaving was something she openly admitted to all her children. He always came home laden with gifts and this became her sole interest in seeing him once a year, wondering what he was going to bring her. Once she had opened all her presents and counted the money he gave her she was impatient for him to be gone again until the following year. There was an old song which had the line, 'You will never miss your mother till she's gone', only she would cruelly, but appropriately, substitute 'father' for 'mother'. I used to dream and pray that Patsy would, at the last moment, decide to take me back to America with him. I might as well have dreamt that Santa Claus was real and currently enjoying his year long sabbatical in the North Pole.

His dubious presence was the only decent present that Patrick and I ever received, from one year to the next. We both hated Christmas with good enough reason. Again there was a 'signal system' set in place on Christmas morning, whereby we were to immediately pass on any toy we received from Patsy until we were both left with nothing. We could only watch our siblings shriek with joy, surrounded by their gifts and the added bonus of our 'unwanted' ones. At some stage it proved too much for one of us and if we started to weep silent, pitiful tears our exasperated father, completely oblivious to the truth, would ask us what on earth was wrong. As usual it was Olive who answered him,

'It's Christmas Day and he's trying to ruin it for the whole family'.

She watched us all day to make sure we didn't dare touch a single toy. The most upsetting part was that although Patsy brought back a lot of stuff from America, the rest of the toys had been especially procured by Patrick and me on our 'shopping' sprees. In hindsight toys would have distracted us from the business of the day. Of course it was just the two of us whose business it was to clear the table and do the massive job of washing and drying the dishes. As you can imagine it took ages. Everything had to be spotless, Olive made sure of that, standing over us, making us re-wash and re-dry the majority of the crockery before she would pronounce it clean.

St Stephen's Day was even more exhausting for us. This was

the day that the children of the town dressed up and went out to sing in order to earn money for the following day, 27 December, when a fair would be set up or else the cinema would show a few good films. It was great fun for kids, well, for other kids at any rate. They could go and sing for a few pence and then go back home to their toys. Patrick and I, on the other hand, were up at 5 am and the money earned from singing for a marathon of at least eighteen hours went towards my father's fare back to America. We were given a steel tin to fill, approximately six inches wide and ten inches deep, which was sealed by soldering lead to prevent us from helping ourselves to our earnings. It was a punishing regime. We were sent out first thing to sing for the early morning shop-keepers and told be home at 1 pm for a nice, hot dinner. That's seven hours of a morning, singing and walking about the town in cold weather. We visited churches, any shop that was open, pubs and neighbours' doorsteps. Naturally she fed us that day, and we were actually allowed to eat it, because of all the money we would bring home. We had a fifteen-minute dinner break – during which our tin was emptied and the contents counted – as we had to be back at the pubs when they started to get busy after the last mass of the day. The next few hours were spent singing our lungs out in the packed pubs. We went back for tea at 6 pm, a particularly exciting occasion for us as it involved cake, biscuits and sweets. At 6.30 pm we were sent back to the pubs, and told to come home at midnight, when the pubs closed. Three times that day we filled the tin, but neither of us were given the slightest idea of how much we made; only our parents seemed relatively satisfied with us, although Olive never failed to grab the chance to tell us that she would make us sorry for the three meals we had eaten.

'When your father is gone you will suffer in the tummy. Only a few days to go now and then you're all mine again!'

And she was true to her word.

The very second after my father's departure she had us naked and back in nappies. Back to being tied, by my arms and legs, to her bed, to prevent me from taking food while she took her afternoon nap. I had no option but to stretch out, as much as I could, on the cool lino of her bedroom floor, dreading what lay ahead of me when she woke up a couple of hours later, refreshed and fighting fit. No single episode sticks out in my memory. Her cruelty was like a merry-go-round, more of the same over and over and over again. The only thing that varied was whether Patrick was beside me or out robbing, on her orders, or downstairs doing the housework. He, on the other hand cannot forget me being kicked about one afternoon as if I was a tattered old rag doll. Because her naps could run to a few hours I would have inevitably wet myself by the time she opened her eyes. Indeed her first words to me were regarding this very subject.

'Well, has Celli pissed his nappy?'

When I answered in the positive she leapt out of the bed and marched into the bathroom where she half-filled the bath using only the cold tap. Just the sound of that running water would have me whimpering out of fear. Next she came in and roughly untied me, ripped off the wet nappy and literally kicked me out of her room, across the landing and into the bathroom. I wished I was a snail or a tortoise, and able to curl up inside a hard shell. Of course it was never enough to grab me by the hair and throw me into the water; she also had to open the window to ensure she was making me as cold as she possibly could. On contact with the water my body would numb all over, the only thing I could feel was the headache I got from the sudden freezing temperature. After some ten minutes or so I was once again dragged by the hair and kicked back out on to the landing, without a chance to dry myself, and into our bedroom, or what Patrick and I preferred to call, just between ourselves, the 'torture chamber', where she locked me in. I took advantage of this interlude to rub myself down with a blanket, curl up and give myself over to sleep. Living in a state of fear, punctuated by horrific events, was exhausting. I was usually asleep within minutes, despite my still trembling body. The previous twenty minutes would never impress themselves on my dreams, instead I invariably dreamt that my lot in life was actually a happy one, I saw myself laughing and smiling, and only when the key in the door woke me from my slumber, and the hunger in my belly hit me forcefully, just before I opened my eyes, did I realise that a nightmare was my reality.

The second part of the punishment was about to begin. She dragged me downstairs and placed me opposite the wall where I was to stare at a specific spot for an unspecified time. It was something akin to today's 'naughty step' or 'bold corner', only infinitely worse than when normal parents punish bad behaviour by making their kid sit by himself for a certain length of time depending on their age, with one minute of punishment representing each year of their lives. For instance a four year old would have to spend no more than four minutes reflecting on his wrong doing. To dull myself to my surroundings I would try my best to reach back into my mind to retrieve my happy fantasy, imagining that my mother's barbaric behaviour was only another dream, a bad one; that I really was as happy-go-lucky as all the other little boys of my acquaintance. After an hour or so of straining to stare at the same spot, my eyes began to betray me by closing. She waited for this moment to leap on me and dig her finger nails into my skin, smashing my reverie, often drawing blood. I still have marks on my face to this day. As soon as she saw the tears well up in my eyes she told me that now I had earned myself a beating for crying like a baby. Patrick was duly sent out to the garden shed to reluctantly select and cut the piece of Patsy's wavin to be used to whip my back, belly, arms and legs.

Perhaps we began to believe that we just were plain bad, or else we simply got used to being the kind of children or victims that people liked to beat up. We were constantly told about our devilment, in every way possible. My mother's frequent farewell to Patrick as he headed off, usually late, for school was the rather pointed,

'You are an ugly bastard. I hope you get run over by a car.'

A variation of this was when she had us take turns at kneeling directly in front of her, of an evening, as she sat in her easy chair, so that she could quite comfortably spit in our faces and tell us exactly how much she hated us.

Thinking ahead, about our futures, she used to drag us about the house by our penises, laughing at our high-pitched screams, telling us that we would never have children if she could help it. Of course we were much too young to understand the link between our shrivelled members and her comments about children that didn't exist.

Olive and Patsy had an awful friend, a very respectable person, who they sometimes invited over to slap me and Patrick around. To my horror, this man was sitting in the front room enjoying tea and cake with our parents the day I was sent home early from school for robbing some money. Perhaps they were waiting especially for me, the principal having already rung ahead to explain what had happened. The money, of course, was to buy food, but nobody, including Patsy, knew that, and I was much too frightened of Olive to tell the truth. So there I was in front of the judge, jury and executioner, all three shouting at me simultaneously. Patsy thumped me a few times, demanding to know why I had stolen the money and then thumped me again when he didn't get an answer. His mate suggested that he might have better luck and asked could he have 'a word with the boy' outside the house. Well, of course he could and if he felt the boy could do with a beating he was to go right ahead. The 'word with the boy' involved the man dragging me up to the locks of the canal, which ran in front of the house, placing his two hands around my neck and squeezing enough to make me sink to the ground, where he continued semi-choking me. When that didn't produce any answers he terrified me by pushing my head into the freezing water, all the while making outlandish, menacing threats that were to be remembered for the future.

When Patrick was eleven years old he arrived home from school one day to find himself named as the main suspect for Olive's missing half crown (about fifteen cents). You will note the repetition in these matters. She undressed him, from head to toe, and told him to go up to the table in the back bedroom. On his way he was to collect a pair of socks and five pairs of her nylon tights, no doubt all stolen by us from Dunnes Stores. She made him open his mouth wide so that she could stuff the socks whole into his mouth, to prevent the neighbours from hearing his screams. Then he was to spread himself across the wooden table, enabling her to use the nylons to tie his wrists and feet to the four legs. She was a strong woman and by the time she tied the last limb to the table he was completely paralysed and defenceless. When the socks threatened to pop out of his mouth, as he continually gagged on them, she used the last pair of tights to hold them tight, by tying them around his head. He could taste the blood where the nylons cut into the sides of his mouth. Producing a large lump of wood, which was maybe three feet long, two inches wide, she beat him.

In his terror he wet himself. When she felt she had hit him enough she untied his legs and arms. He fell off the table on to the floor, which is how she noticed the pool of urine. She dragged him to his feet and forced him to bend over the table, rubbing his face into his urine. The cuts on his mouth sizzled and when he tried to stand up straight he felt his legs go from under him. Allowing him to slump lifelessly to the floor she headed for the bathroom and started running the cold water. His body was covered with marks from the tights and scores of developing bruises, all the colour of a depressed rainbow, from the wooden club. The cold water would soon sort them out. After his bath, where she had physically held his body down in the water, she flung him wet and naked into our bedroom, locking the door. As he drifted off to a desperate sleep he heard her starting on the six-year-old me, demanding her half-crown while reefing the clothes off me, bellowing for the wooden club.

She had trained us to steal for her, feeding us as a reward, showing us the way to her heart. She alone knew our capabilities, and could be confident that our primary motivation was her alone, that we just wanted to make her happy with us. Nevertheless there was no basking in the knowledge that ultimately all we had to do was nip down to Dunnes or over the Clara Bridge, because our talent was only another excuse to batter us. If anything went missing, or was merely mislaid in the house, Olive could cheerfully blame us because of the sins we were committing for her. She never hit us for nothing; instead she would out of necessity create a situation in which we had wronged her in some way. This could mean anything from accusing me of robbing my sister's purse despite the fact that I was in school, because she knew I did rob stuff for her, or else giving us an impossible household chore to perform where inevitable failure would inevitably lead to a brutal beating.

She always imagined, or perhaps it would be more truthful to say she always *liked* to imagine, that people were looking down on her and that she had to go to battle to avenge herself. This was certainly true of the elderly couple who had the misfortune to live next door to us. Theirs was a hard-working family; they owned a small sweet shop right up the street from us, and were reasonably well-to-do which meant, as far as Olive was concerned, that they were full of themselves and needed to be taken down a peg or three. Of course it was Patrick and me, not Olive, who had to scream and curse at them, give them the finger whenever the opportunity presented itself, or throw stones at their windows. We were set upon these gentle folk who had done us no harm. Patrick and I were regularly sent to scavenge from the apple trees in their back garden – and in the day time so that a point was made in the broadest terms possible. We knew they were watching us take their fruit, but they never once called out to us. Either they had an idea of what was going on in our house or else they didn't dare initiate a confrontation with our mother. They complained only once to her, about our calling them names; she told them to 'Fuck off!' At some stage they were obliged to put a steel mesh on their back windows so that we wouldn't break them. They were the nicest people and we were thoroughly ashamed of ourselves, but what could we do? We had our orders.

The day my sister's purse went missing is certainly high on my list of the most excruciating experience. My sister was long gone by the time I was being accused of robbing her purse. Olive was paddling my bare body with the 'Cheese Please!' board, a solid plank of varnished wood, about six inches wide and twelve inches long, with a long wooden handle made from a one inch thick butcher block, which hit harder than any other piece of wood. Even the wavin, which stung, was preferable to this particular weapon. The pain on impact was tremendous. She beat and kicked me for what seemed like hours before she would explain what it was all about. Apparently my sister, who was by now a wife and mother, had visited our house that morning and now her purse was gone. Olive fancied I must have snuck home early from school, tiptoed into the house, robbed the purse and returned to school before I was seen. Well, our home was not a place I would escape to in the middle of the day and I hadn't known about my sister coming to visit.

I tried to reason with her, but found myself bundled into an armchair in the living room. She turned the chair around so that I was facing the wall, and tied my wrists and feet to the chair arms and legs, with a tea towel around my mouth to gag me against making too much noise. For the next six hours or so she wouldn't let anyone else into that room, she was my only visitor, marching in to whip me with a belt, every twenty minutes or so, wanting me to confess to my crime. At one point she swung the belt so tightly that the buckle caught me in the face, ripping my flesh. I've a mark there to this day. The pain turned into shock and suddenly the belt stopped hurting even as she was lashing it against me. I must have given up, however, because I admitted taking the purse – probably out of sheer exhaustion. It was sometime between 8 and 9 pm when she untied my battered, bruised and bleeding body from the chair.

I had formed a plan to run away and when she told me I had one more chance to explain what I did with the purse, I told her that I had hidden it up by the train station. My only hope for escape was her sending me out to fetch it. Unfortunately this didn't happen. Instead Michael, my older brother, was told to put on his coat and Olive dragged us both out into the cold night to get the damn purse. She kept a firm grip on me and when I couldn't locate the evidence I timidly suggested that someone else must have taken it from the field. I have never felt so trapped in my life. When we got back to the house she beat me for what seemed like a couple of hours before I could ease my body into bed. This time I told her that I had left it in my desk at school, planning to run away the following day. I wanted to die and begged God, telling Him that if He really loved me He'd take me straight to Heaven. Once again my plan backfired the following morning, when she refused to let me go to school because I was so badly bruised and marked.

My sister arrived back at the house a few hours later and Olive told her that her purse was in my desk. She said that she would go to the school immediately and let Olive know if it was there or not. True to her word she rang about an hour later and said that yes she had found the purse and nothing had been taken from it. Which was, of course, impossible. Speaking to this sister recently I asked her about the matter. She told me that she had actually found her purse at the top of the stairs in our house. Perhaps Olive had lifted it herself in order to permit herself to batter me as she did.

Our sisters and brothers were terrified of Olive's rages. Most of the time, she sent them out of the house, when the mood was upon her. When they were there they would beg her, in vain, to stop beating us. I think Padre Pio himself would have been hard pressed to intervene successfully when she was upon us.

After a beating had left us covered in bruises we were locked away from the eyes of the world for days on end. Typically we weren't allowed to eat or drink unless one of us looked like we might need to go to a hospital. Because the bathroom was off limits – in case it gave us an opportunity to get some water – we were forced to come up with an alternative way to answer the call of Mother Nature. One of us had an old boot which we both pissed and shat into and then hid up the chimney breast. There must have been a smell, but I honestly don't remember. Her paranoia about us escaping and, perhaps, showing off our bruises to another adult, stretched to how she tucked us into bed at night. She would actually bind us in. Our arms were pinioned to our sides as she wrapped us up tightly in a sheet, folding it around our body as if she was rolling a joint. Then she thoroughly tucked in our outer blanket, deep into the sides of the mattress. Our fingertips, toes, neck and facial muscles were the only movable parts after she had finished. You can appreciate now how I wet my bed so much.

If she had a beating to give and she hadn't the time or interest to grab the 'Cheese Please!' board; or she just couldn't be bothered waiting for Patrick to select and cut a piece of wavin or a lump of wood; or perhaps Patsy had taken all his good belts to America; she would use something that was a bit more personal. Maybe you have seen that film *Single White Female*, where the utterly psychotic female character goes on a jealous rampage, killing the protagonist's lover by stabbing him in the eye with one of her stilettos. When one of our sisters was sick and vomited over the bottom of the stairs Olive called for Patrick to clean it up. He refused, completely repulsed by the mess and the smell. She grabbed him by the hair and pushed his face into the vomit, holding him still by placing her foot on the back of his neck. Not surprisingly he cleaned up the sick, but she wasn't finished with him yet. For daring to cheek her she removed one of her high heels and aimed for his skull. To this day Patrick has a scar in the back of his head where she plunged the shoe into him.

# Part Two:
# Patrick

OFFALY COUNTY COUNCIL 40

PUBLIC HEALTH DEPARTMENT
COURTHOUSE
TULLAMORE

REF.

9th January, 1970.

Hospitaller Order of St. John of God,
Child Guidance Clinic,
Orwell Road,
Rathgar,
Dublin.

Re:- Patrick Doyle, 3, Pearse Park,
Tullamore, your ref: 753/10/222.

Dear Brother

The abovementioned attended the Child Guidance Clinic on 21/11/1969 and to date I have not received a report. Will you kindly let me have a report.

Psychiatric Social Worker at the Clinic rang to-day and she informed me that she wishes Patrick to attend again and also his brother Kenneth. Apparently the father mentioned about Kenneth when he attended with Patrick on 21st November.

I have requested the father to let me know if he will agree to bring Patrick and Kenneth to the clinic if appointments are made and I will write to you again if he agrees.

# Runaway

*'In 1965 Mr Doyle's parents contacted the ISPCC in Athlone because Patrick was obviously hungry and was taking food out of the neighbouring bins.'*
(Case History, 31 October 1969)

I ran away a lot. Sometimes it was the middle of winter and all I'd have on me was a worn, thin, tee-shirt and pants. I'd grab clothes from neighbour's lines and, in the early days, would stop confused a few minutes away from our house, wondering where on earth I was going to. But at least I was away from her, the woman who had told me repeatedly for as long as I could remember that she hoped I would die soon because she hated the very sight of me. My initial hiding place was our neighbour's coal shed, which allowed me access to their bins as well as ours. I was afraid to stay in the house, but I was also afraid to go too far from it. When it got dark I hid myself behind a mound of turf, much too frightened to relax, never mind sleep. Then at about 5 am I'd leave my largely uncomfortable sanctuary and make my way to the railway bridge where I would spend the entire day watching my house, looking out – I think – for visiting Gardaí. After a few days I went home again. Remember I was only about ten or eleven years of age. The welcome I received depended on whether I had come back via Dunnes Stores or not. If I had, the beating, specifically for running away, would be postponed for twenty-four hours or so.

I remember my first bad beating. I think I was maybe six or seven years old and I was trying to accomplish that first grown-up challenge, tying my own shoe laces. My mother was watching me, making me nervous. After a few seconds she barked out the 'biblical' command,

'Don't use thee elbows!'

'I'm not mammy.' (In truth, I had no idea what she was talking about.)

'Are you trying to do my head in? You have just tied your shoes with your elbows and you're standing there telling me you weren't.'

What stands out especially for me is the effect the stress my abnormal home life had on me. At the time I couldn't understand what was making me so determined on hurting myself. Was I not in enough pain already? I scared myself when I spun out of control. I didn't want to be like my mother. Sometimes I would chomp down on the inside of my mouth, or even my tongue, until I could taste the sweetness of my own blood.

Other times I would punch myself, over and over again, in the stomach or the face. I developed a habit of head-butting the wall of the 'torture chamber' until I could almost see stars. Another unhealthy pastime was pulling the hairs out of my head, fistfuls at a time. It is only as an adult that I recognised the signs of severe stress, made partly worse by the fact that I was the older brother. It was one thing to undergo the battering that I did, and the equally brutal, and constant, mental torture, it was quite another to have to watch my little brother being kicked around the house, like he was some sort of weightless beach ball, or dragged across a room by his penis. There are five years between us, which seemed like a huge gap when I was eleven years old and he was a frighteningly small six-year-old tot. I was consumed with fear for my situation, but I was also guilt-ridden by the fact that I was too scared to help Ken. All I did was watch in horror. I watched her jump on his leg and I heard the snap as she threatened to break his other leg if he didn't stand up immediately and stop crying. Again, as an adult, I understand now that there was absolutely nothing I could have done to save him. It was because of him that I aborted my most serious suicide attempt; the idea of intentionally leaving him totally alone in her clutches was more than I could bear. As it was all I did was worry about him when I did manage to run away.

Over the next few months my courage grew alongside my dread of Olive, so much so that I was able to exchange the coal shed for the freezing, roofless ruin of Srah Castle. I was always scared, scared of being alone, scared of the dark nights, scared of possible ghosts or blood-thirsty murderers. But I had to do something to break the cycle of Olive's hatred for me. Quite a number of my adventures ended in the worst possible way when I was brought back to the house courtesy of the Gardaí.

Thanks to all the thieving I was doing, my reputation was growing in the local police station. When you're stealing to eat, and therefore stealing seven days a week, you have to accept that you are going to get caught a certain number of times. And Olive always put on a wonderful performance for the guards, it really was something to behold. Whether I got caught running away or helping myself to God knows what in Dunnes Stores she would be ready waiting for her cue. Turning first to the guards who were escorting me she would lament:

'Why is he doing this to me?'

When all eyes steered grimly in my direction she would then address me, her co-star, with the same question.

'Why are you doing this to me? I don't understand. Why? Why? What is making you do this? Is it something I'm doing wrong?'

To which I would always answer,

'No mammy, it has nothing to do with you.'

Because I was good little boy.

✉ ✉ ✉

I was in trouble so often that it often seemed to me that all adults were against me, so when a friend of my parents seemed to like me, I wanted to trust him.

He asked my parents to let me do a bit of work for him in exchange for some pocket money. Of course Olive and Patsy agreed so I was given a key to his house and asked to do a few jobs. One day when I had been painting for him, he came home from work, complimented me on my work, and then suggested that I take a bath before I went home. I was relieved because I had paint in my hair and on my arms and hands, and I knew that Olive would probably have a fit if she thought I was bringing a speck of paint into her house. There was also the fact that there is no way on earth that she'd let me bathe in hot water so I was very grateful for the chance to do so now. He laid a bath towel on the floor beside the bath, just inside the door, and told me that I could leave my clothes there in a pile. Naturally I thought nothing of it and did as he told me. When I had scrubbed myself clean I stood up, in the bath, looking for both the towel and my clothes, but they were nowhere to be seen. That was strange. Thanks to my mother's training I was very mindful of dropping water all over the floor, but I stepped out on one leg to look around the door for my clothes. He was sitting in a chair with the bath towel that he had gotten for me. There was a strange look on his face and I instinctively wanted to cover myself.

'Come here to me. I'll dry you.'

It was more of a question than a statement and I just said 'no'. I was embarrassed and retreated unsteadily back into the bathroom, from where I heard the front door slam a few minutes later and then his car starting up. I found my clothes and dragged them on to my still dripping wet body, trying to understand what had just happened. He hadn't left me any money either, which upset me apart from his bizarre behaviour, so I helped myself. Earlier that day I noticed a plastic lunch box filled with coins and I decided now that I had earned them. Figuring that this was probably the last time I'd be in his house after what happened, I grabbed the whole box and left.

A couple of days later I was hiding out in the little makeshift hut that I had put together in Offaly Street, just a few planks of mouldy wood propped up against a wall. Not many people knew about it but he did. I heard him calling my name and reluctantly came out to meet him. When he asked me about the box of coins I told him that I didn't know what he was talking about. He ordered me to get into the car; I sat into the passenger's seat and he drove us to the GAA club, just opposite the hospital, where he pulled in, telling me that we needed to have a little talk. He asked me again about the money, but I continued to deny all knowledge about it. It had only amounted to a few quid and was long gone, spent on a feast of crisps and biscuits for Ken and myself. I felt very uncomfortable in the car, the stench of the flowery air freshener was upsetting my stomach and I wished he would open a window. The interior seemed to shrink as I sat there listening to him talking in a low, intimate tone, all the while staring straight at me. Nobody had ever spoken to me so softly before. I was tense, all of my limbs gathered together, waiting for the punch that never came. To my horror my eyes welled up with tears as he quietly lectured me about the need for us to trust one another, after all there was plenty more painting to be done and he also had other jobs that needed doing about the house. We sat there in silence for a while and then he asked if I wanted to finish the painting, driving us back to his house when I answered 'yes'. He fetched all the brushes, opened the can of paint that I was half-way through and stood up the step ladder for me so that I could reach the top of the walls. I took up a brush, dipped it gently into the can and took a few steps up the ladder, absorbed in working out which was the best way to slant the brush against the wall. Suddenly he was on the rung below me, both his arms around my waist, asking me if I would like to kiss him. Appalled I stammered out 'no'. He got down and, once again, strode out of his house leaving me behind shaking in disbelief.

⊠ ⊠ ⊠

One time when things in the Doyle household became too much, I walked and hitchhiked over a hundred miles to Mayo, hardly aware of where I was going, eaten up with guilt at the thought of poor Ken languishing at home. Another time I managed to stay away for six weeks. I got a job with the local blacksmith, telling him that I needed to make some money for my mother for Christmas. This much was true. I also told him that I wanted it to be a surprise so he couldn't tell any of my family that I was working for him. Every day he asked after my family, not realising that I was spending the nights in his forge, washing in the local river and stealing bread and milk from doorsteps. I saved my wages over the six weeks in order to present it to Olive. It was a snowy 21 December when I decided it was time to make my return. My head was ferociously itchy, I was in dire need of a bath and my clothes were in shreds. I must have made a sorry sight when I nervously knocked on our backdoor. As soon as she opened the door I told her I had money for her. She let me in. Everyone was in the kitchen, including Patsy, who was home for his Christmas visit. He shocked me by bursting into tears as soon as he saw me. I was covered in lice and dirt, and all my clothes had to be immediately taken out to be burned. It felt good to be back. And maybe Olive was just a little glad to see me, even if she only regarded my return from a purely commercial angle.

The next morning she told me I could have a lovely dinner that day if I did her Christmas 'shopping' for her. She had a long list, two Dunnes Stores trolleys' worth. When I brought all the food back to her she told me that I needed to get her a Christmas present so I went back into the town and stole a holy picture for her. I was sent back out a third time to nick 'Santa' toys for my brothers and sisters. By the time I was sitting down to my dinner I thought my work was done. The cupboards and the fridge were full and all the presents were hidden upstairs. But Olive had other plans. She told me I was taking the train to Dublin the following day, so that I could steal some handbags. The idea of travelling by myself to the capital scared me but I wouldn't say no to her.

'All we need now is a few shillings and then we won't be stuck for anything. And if you could get a few more toys that would be great.'

The next day I headed off rather reluctantly to the station for the 12.30 train. I didn't want to go to Dublin and I didn't want to steal anything else, but I certainly couldn't return empty handed. I needed money. If I had my own money I could buy stuff instead of stealing handbags. Suddenly I knew what I had to do. I decided to break into my school and empty the phone box, something I had done several times before. To my relief it was overflowing with coins that I wrapped up in the school flag. There was no time to count it so I climbed back out through the broken office window and continued on my way, thrilled with myself. On reaching Dublin I made my way to the Bank of Ireland where I asked the cashier for a bundle of plastic bags. After that I spent a leisurely hour beside the River Liffey, counting out the coins into their respective bags so that I could exchange them for notes. There was over a £100 which made me feel a lot more confident about walking around the bustling city. For starters I went to a café for a hot dinner and then I made my way to the Phoenix Park to see the deer and the President's house. Somehow I managed to infiltrate a group of carol singers that arrived to sing outside Áras an Uachtaráin. Then it was time for me to head back into the city centre and do my shopping. I thoroughly enjoyed selecting toys for my sisters and brothers; dolls that could cry and drink their own bottle of water, planes, dinky cars, Sindy dolls and pyjamas – of course there was no point in buying anything for Ken or myself. It was much more relaxing without the constant worry of being caught thieving. The shops were warm and busy while the Christmas songs kept everyone cheerful and smiling. When I went for my evening train I had bags and bags of purchases that I would have to pretend I stole – or she'd explode – and I still had £50 in cash for Olive. I was quite sure that I had earned myself another dinner when I got home.

So it was quite a nasty shock to find an outraged Olive waiting for me, screaming at me that the police had been at the house over my breaking into the school. I tried to tell her no, I had gone straight to Dublin, just like I was supposed to. She kicked me to the ground and then rang the police to tell them I had come home at long last. I was told to get my story straight.

'You tell them that I sent you to buy milk and bread hours ago and you're only getting back now.'

When the garda arrived, he tried to get me to admit that I had broken into the school, but I kept denying it. What he didn't realise was that he didn't frighten me, but Olive did. She was determined to cover her tracks, not that anyone would have ever suspected the truth.

'Tell the officer how long ago it was that I sent you to the shops.'

He never actually mentioned the phone box that I'd taken the money from, just the window I had broken to enter the school, not that I would admit that much to him. He eventually gave up, having to settle for informing me that I was a disgrace to my parents. Which I was used to hearing. When he left she beat me for bringing the police to our door. I was locked into the bedroom while she collected all the presents together, to wrap them downstairs. She never thanked me, never fed me; I found myself planning my next jaunt from this hell hole.

✉ ✉ ✉

When I was fifteen, my mother went out of her way to embarrass me into isolation from other children. She would turn up outside my school and wait for me to stream out with the rest of my noisy, fiercely independent and struggling-to-be-an-adult peers. Invariably I was the one lagging behind, in the background. After all it wasn't like I had a nice home or a hot dinner to go back to. Out of all the hundreds of swarming parents and kids she alone knew how I would dread the sight of her standing there, smiling sweetly in my general direction as if she was delighted to see me. And no doubt she was delighted because my arrival allowed her to carry on with the humiliation. Taking my reluctant hand in hers she would loudly proclaim to my giggling classmates,

'See how Patrick has to be collected like this. I have to hold his hand or he'd only try to rob something from the shops on the way home.'

This much was true of course. I had to rob something in

order to survive the evening without a thrashing and be allowed to eat some bread. By now I was being wolf- whistled and kids were pointing me out to their friends. However she wasn't done yet. She had another bit of ridiculous information to impart which would seal my fate regarding the attitude of the school population.

'Would you believe that Patrick has to wear a nappy to bed every night because he keeps wetting the bed? Isn't that only shocking?'

Yep, it certainly was.

# 'My Days Were Numbered'

When I was sixteen Mother Nature took over and I found myself feeling a little more confident around my mother. Accordingly she became somewhat wary, as I went about the business of being a sixteen-year-old fella, and was obliged to switch tactics. I had plenty of friends to knock about with and we were into the usual teenager stuff – that is, trying to work up a healthy appetite for alcohol and women. In that order. It did me no end of good to find myself the object of quite a few girls' affections and I was never short of a girlfriend. The only problem was the brevity of these largely innocent relationships. As soon as my mother found out who I was dating she would find a way to let the girl know that I couldn't be trusted, that I had been in trouble with the police all my life. There was one particular girl that I fell quite heavily for and I managed to keep her a secret for a few months. One afternoon I met her after school as planned and she told me that we couldn't see each other anymore as my mother had actually written her a letter to say I was bad news and that she should stay away from me for her own sake.

In hindsight Olive must have been looking around for a way to be rid of me. No doubt my days in the house were numbered after I lost my temper with her, the first time I had ever done so. I came home one evening to find her in the middle of a typically frenzied attack on Ken. He was sobbing silently, naked and rolled up in a ball at her feet; meanwhile she was kicking and thumping him on his little back, as if she was trying to make him bounce like a basketball. It was a scene I had witnessed so many times and had been too frightened to intervene, but now I felt a new sensation. Some kind of seething tension was forming in my gut, in the tips of my fingers, and it was slowly edging its way towards my throat; anger. The child in me stood apart and watched the sixteen-year-old roar at the monster that was his mother,

'Stop it! Leave him alone!'

Without even thinking about it, because if I had I would never have done it, I picked up a Pyrex dish from the table and threw it in her direction. It smashed against the ground, the noise of the shattering stopping everyone in their tracks. I didn't hang around for her reaction. Maybe I was afraid of what I'd do had I stayed any longer; therefore I ran from the house and stayed away for several weeks.

I was stealing all around me at this point, whether I was in Tullamore or not, trying desperately to keep Olive happy. As a result

I was getting caught a lot more and eventually ended up in Mountjoy Jail. I was still a minor and due back in court, but the Juvenile Detention Centre was full so I was brought to the top jail in Dublin where I spent the next two weeks. There I met the governor (now a good friend of mine) and was handed a pillow case, which contained underclothes, two sheets, one pillow case and the infamous bar of soap. Everyone treated me well; I must have looked so tiny and innocent compared to some of the other occupants. When my case came up the judge no doubt thought he was being very indulgent by letting me go free. In fact I was bitterly disappointed that I couldn't stay in Mountjoy any longer. Don't get me wrong, my prison cell was dirty and cold, with only a worn out potty to go in, but still it was one hundred per cent better than living with Olive. Think about it. I received three square meals a day and I was allowed to sleep the night through: no beatings, no laundry, no freezing baths to minimise the colours of my bruises. This would be the first of four prison terms that I would serve. I was a model prisoner, even if I say so myself. I got on with everyone and even availed, later on, of the educational opportunities. My frequent absences and expulsions from schools had left me with very poor skills in writing and reading, but I was determined now to make up for lost time. My fellow prisoners found my love for being behind bars rather endearing. In those days the buildings were old and damp and everyone looked forward to getting outside again. But not me.

When I was released I immediately went on another crime spree. I was running out of time in Tullamore, and I must have felt it in the air. My thieving was more serious now, reflecting the fact that Olive's tastes were a bit more sophisticated than they used to be. The days of stealing Waterford Crystal from a shop window were pure child's play compared to the boldness of what I was getting up to – breaking into nightclubs, pubs and shops in the dead of night and taking larger sums of money than ever before. I ran off to Cork and, following some ludicrous thieving, ended up spending a very pleasant month in the jail there. Sometimes I wished I could just stay in jail forever instead of having to go through the hassle of being sent back to my mother who was just as desperate to see the back of me, as I was of her. Perhaps it would be fair to say that I wanted to get caught, that I was doing my utmost to be put away forever.

And then it came.

When I was seventeen years old, my mother threw some of my clothes in a plastic bag and brought them out to the car, telling me to jump in the back seat. When I asked where we were going my father only said that the three of us were going for a drive. I wasn't so sure. Something was up. They were much too quiet for my liking, but I did as I was told. When we had left Tullamore behind Olive turned around to me.

'Now you're a very sick boy, but we know a man who will make you better. It just might take a few days so you'll have to sleep over.'

To be honest this sounded alright to me, in fact I was glad to be sleeping elsewhere for a while. At least they fed you in hospital and took care of you. I assumed it was a normal hospital I was going to and relaxed to gawk out the window. Eventually, we arrived at a large red-brick building with pretty gardens. We stopped in front of the reception area. Olive stayed in the car while Patsy and I headed inside to the office. I had to sign some papers, something to do with whether I owned property or not. There were other forms too; I just signed them as I was told to – thus signing myself unknowingly into a psychiatric hospital. The doctor kept me talking while Patsy snuck out without saying goodbye. At the very last minute I happened to glance out a window and see the car retreating down the driveway. I was led to a ward with about sixteen beds and told which one was mine. The old man in the bed next to mine was constantly involved in a loud dialogue with God. He scared me. After a few nights I was moved into a bigger ward of about twenty beds. I found myself wishing to be back beside that first guy when I found myself under attack from another elderly man. Every night, after the staff turned out the lights, this old guy who everyone called 'Grandad' would crawl into my bed and try to climb on top of me.

How could my parents have brought me to this place? Did they know what was going on with this miserable bunch of people who appeared to be one and all dangerously mad? I spent most of the time utterly terrified, and with good reason. Complaining about Grandad invading my bed got me nowhere. He was allowed to continue sleeping in the bed next to mine, and when I was under attack an orderly would wearily call out:

'Oh, would you ever just leave him alone.'

Which had no effect whatsoever.

Worse was yet to come when I was taken down to the wash room one night, with about eleven other patients. We were told to strip and wait our turn to get into the one large tub in the centre of the room. Only some of the men jumped in together and, watched by the staff, began to wildly masturbate themselves and one another. Someone shouted a half-hearted 'Stop!', but that was it. Then I had to climb into this same water and wash myself. But worse was yet to come.

A few days later I went down for a bath and just as I stepped out I was pushed against a locker that held brushes and cleaning equipment. Another patient, about six foot tall and maybe eighteen stone in weight, had me pinned naked up against the wall. He was actually foaming at the mouth, screaming at me;

'Do it! Do it! Do it! Do it!'

When I asked, nobody could tell me how long I would be staying there. My family never visited me once, which, I suppose, was to be expected. It turns out that I had also signed myself up for a course of electroshock therapy, a typical treatment for severe depression. I tried my best to escape several times, but it was impossible. Most of the other patients frightened me with their wailing, wanton defecating and unpredictable behaviour. There were others who did nothing more than lie silently, for hours, on the ground, completely lost to the world. I remember one man who spent his day covering himself and his cell in his own shit, after which he would kneel on his window sill looking out across the gardens, dreaming, no doubt, of being free once more.

We were locked in twenty-four hours a day. I craved to feel fresh air on my face. One of the patients was given the job of washing the windows and I used to bribe him with my dessert to try to open one of the heavy roller windows, but he could never manage it. Nevertheless he still demanded his payment, and if I refused to give it to him he would spit in my dinner and roar abuse at me.

I was released four months later. Patsy came to take me home. My mother's face was a picture when I walked through our front door. Her plan hadn't worked out as she would have liked it to. It was as plain as the plain nose on her face that I was back far too soon.

It would be many years later that I would discover how an eminent doctor finally wrote to the board of the hospital, emphatically calling for my release because there was nothing wrong with me.

# Crossing the Irish Sea

After my release I was soon back to my criminal ways once more. I never, ever wanted to set foot in that hospital again, but I genuinely didn't mind going back to prison. Possibly with this very thought in mind it wasn't too long before I ended up back in front of a judge. By now I had a bit of a prison record as a young re-offender and the judge decided to be a bit harder on me this time, to mend my ways for good. I was sentenced to be held in St Patrick's Juvenile Delinquent Centre, which was right next door to that lovely place Mountjoy, on the North Circular Road in Dublin. I didn't like St Patrick's as much as the other places I had been in. The staff members were not as friendly and it actually seemed a lot rougher. I suppose I had been treated like a baby when I was in Mountjoy whereas here I was one of the oldest. Also my stay was a lot longer.

It was about a year later, at seven one morning, that I was told to pack my kit and come down to reception. I was being released along with twelve other men, all of varying ages. I could hardly believe my luck and half expected to be told that there had been some sort of mistake, especially as my name was the last to be called. A social worker met me and brought me to the Governor's office, where I was told that yes I was being released, but no, I wasn't going back to Tullamore just yet. Instead I was going to an address in Huddersfield, in West Yorkshire, England, where, they had been told, the woman of the house was expecting me and a job had been lined up by my mother. The governor handed me a ferry ticket for Dublin to Liverpool, along with a ticket for a train connection to Huddersfield. Well, I had heard of England, but that was about it. I was also given a small brown envelope with my name on it. Inside was £4 for my trip. The only downside was that I had to wear the same clothes I had on me and they were mightily stained and creased. I was thanked by the governor for being such a good prisoner and never causing a moment of trouble. He shook my hand and wished me the best of luck for the future.

The social worker brought me outside to his car. He was going to drive me to the North Wall to catch the 9.30 am ferry. My head was in a whirl and I struggled to understand both that I was free at last and that I was leaving Ireland within the next couple of hours. It was kind of hard to take in all at once. As we neared the port my stomach began to churn. You would think by now that I might have got tired of being scared of everything; that I might have just been glad to get out, but I was now heading off into the complete unknown, all alone as usual. The social worker parked the car and explained that his job was to get me on the ferry, therefore as soon as I boarded I was to make my way to the top deck, at the rear of the boat, so that he could see me, letting him know that he had carried out his duty to the bitter end. I did what I was told, I waved at the only person to witness my leaving my home and country for the very first time and it lifted me a little when he returned my tentative gesture. I was seventeen years old.

✉ ✉ ✉

Ireland never seemed so precious to me as she fell behind into the distance. My heart ached with the thought of never seeing any of my friends, familiar places or even my family again. So I did what most fellas would do in my situation: I went in search of a strong drink. Old habits, as they say, die hard: I nicked a bottle of gin that was sitting on a table and found a quiet spot away from the rest of the passengers. This is the last I remember of the boat trip as the next thing I know I'm waking up, one day later, in a Liverpool train station. The journey to Huddersfield was a long and hungry one since I hadn't eaten a thing in almost two days. It was after 11 pm when the train dropped me off. I asked directions to my accommodation, which turned out to be a three-mile walk. Exhaustion was setting in when I finally knocked on number fourteen in a quiet council estate. I was a little thrown by the fact that all the lights were off, although it was well after midnight; perhaps she had given up on me. It seemed like a long time before a pleasant-faced woman opened the door. She looked mightily surprised to find me on her doorstep, but I was glad to hear her Irish accent.

'Hello, I'm Patrick Doyle. I was sent here about a job and a place to stay.'

She looked even more surprised then and I began to have a bad feeling in the pit of my stomach.

'I'm sorry love but I think you have the wrong house.'

I checked the number on her door again; yes, number fourteen; that was right. Too tired to think I handed her the sheet of paper with her address on it and told her my mother had sent me over here for a job and a place to stay. I could feel hot tears starting to gather and I blinked hard to make them disappear. The woman handed me back the paper in total bewilderment, explaining that she honestly had no idea what this was all about. Nevertheless she held the door open and invited me to come in anyway, telling me that I was probably hungry after my journey. It was the first time in a long while that anyone had showed me such kindness. Bleary-eyed I followed her into her tiny kitchen where she made me sit down and watch her prepare a supper for me. Naturally enough she asked me a lot of questions about my family background. As soon as I mentioned Olive she stopped what she was doing.

'Oh Patrick, I know her! But I haven't seen or heard of her in years and years. Sure the last time I saw her she was only a little slip of a thing.'

I was mortified. Obviously Olive had set me up just to be

rid of me; anything to stop me from coming back to her house. Maybe she reckoned on the kindness of her old friend though I'm sure she didn't care enough about me to wonder what kind of a reaction I got when I finally reached the address she gave me. Seeing the distress in my face the woman, who had gotten out of her bed to answer her door and was now making scrambled eggs at almost one in the morning, for a strange boy she had only just met, told me simply,

'Don't worry son, you can stay here until you get yourself settled.'

And that was that. I shared a small bedroom with her twin sons, Tommy and Billy, and was pretty much treated like one of the family. Of course there was no job lined up for me, but it was only a matter of days before I began working for an Irish construction firm, digging miles of trenches around west Yorkshire with other Irish lads. The work was tough, especially in bad weather, but I found it liberating in a way. I had a job to do every day, for which I got paid, and it felt good to work hard at something honest, something that helped me fall into an exhausted sleep as soon as my head touched the pillow. For the first time ever my domestic life was one of ease. Now all I had to do was forget about the past. No mean feat. I started drinking socially with the guys I worked with. We worked hard and played even harder. At first it was a few pints at the weekend, but after a while I noticed how much easier it was to forget about everything else when I was drunk. I was great fun when I was drunk, making people laugh, singing songs. You would never think I had been hated, battered and starved by my mother or raped by mad men in a mental hospital.

The weekend drinks spilled into the evenings leading up to the weekend, until it became every evening. The few pints were rapidly exchanged for something stronger; rum, whiskey or brandy, depending on how I was feeling – all straight, hold the ice. I craved the sensation these spirits produced, how they scorched my tongue as I held a mouthful to savour it, blasting the back of my throat before burning their way through to the pit of my stomach. Pure unadulterated Heaven! Nobody could understand why I had to get so drunk every evening. Only I knew what I was doing but I wasn't telling. I had found an enjoyable way to numb the pain.

# 'My Present, My Future, My World'

In time I gave up digging trenches to wash wool in a mill in Huddersfield town and I also got myself a tiny, poky flat that I loved because it was all mine, my very own sanctuary from the rest of the world. For the next twelve months or so my life was uneventful. I did my best not to think too much about anything. Beyond the routine of drinking and sleeping around the long shifts at the mill I had no other plans, no thoughts nor ambitions for my future. Something, however, was starting to give and it took me a while to figure out what it was. For all the easy camaraderie I enjoyed in the pubs I was feeling lonely for Ireland. I can't explain exactly what it was that I was missing. To be sure I had plenty of Irish friends where I was, but it just wasn't the same. England, when it came right down to it, was a different country and I felt that difference keenly. I wanted to go back, but not to Tullamore. I decided upon Cork city, my favourite city in the whole world. Once my decision was made I sold the contents of my flat for £25, which was the only money I had.

In August 1978 I took off to Huddersfield train station to buy a one-way ticket to Cork. The boat fare was £7, but the only crossing to Cork was from Swansea in Wales, and that train journey was £28. The only thing to do was hitch-hike my way to Wales. My determination to get to Cork would not be thwarted by any such obstacle. It took me three days and I had to sleep rough, but I got there in the end. A chatty truck driver dropped me off outside the Swansea train station on a beautiful summer afternoon. There wasn't a cloud in the pristine blue sky as I thanked my final chauffeur and looked around for a pub. By now all I had on me was my ticket and a two pence piece. I was hungry and incredibly thirsty with the heat of the day so I wanted to go to the gents in order to drink a mouthful of tap water. Once I boarded the ferry I could steal some food. I hadn't stolen anything in a while, but I was sure it would all come back to me. The first bar I saw was The Pullman and I went inside to ask for directions to the ferry port. An old gentleman told me how to get there, it wasn't too far away, and he also made an innocent suggestion which was to change the course of my life forever more.

'That's an Irish accent, isn't it? Yeah, I thought so. You should try the Irish bar at the end of Wind Street. That's where all the Irish men drink.'

I thanked him for the directions and headed down High Street onto Wind Street. Before I had even reached the building I heard the familiar sounds of one of my favourite songs streaming out of the open windows of the Burrows Arms, 'The Green, Green Grass of Home' sung by that most famous of Welshmen, Tom Jones. I had to go in. It was a tiny place and it was packed to the rafters with happy Irish and Welshmen who were singing along with Tom at the top of their voices. The atmosphere was amazing and I fervently wished I could stay and have something more than water out of a sink tap. But I couldn't. I went into the gents, had my fill of vaguely unpleasant tasting water and headed to the door. As I opened it a young boy stepped in; he couldn't have been more than fourteen years old. He smiled at me and I asked him for directions to the port.

'Sure just wait for me outside. I'll have a chat with you after I use the toilet.'

When he came out he told me to wait a minute and off he went to the bar. He returned with a pint of Guinness that he had bought me. I was extremely grateful for his kindness although I really would have preferred a plate of food as I was weak with the hunger. But you can't look a gift horse in the mouth and all that. I was more than glad to have a reason to stay a while longer. For one thing the girl serving behind the bar was one of the prettiest I had ever seen. And the Guinness she poured wasn't too bad either. Plus I still had an hour to kill before I could board the ferry. The boy, whose name was Eddie, explained that the bar girl was his sister and that his father, an Irishman, owned the pub. He asked what I was up to so I told him that I had made the decision to return to Ireland for good, filling him in on what I had been doing in Liverpool and Huddersfield. Then he asked me outright had I any money and I replied truthfully that no, I was penniless. God bless him, but he went and got me another pint. The drink was going to straight to my head, thanks to my empty stomach, and I was also conscious of time ticking away. This time he told me that his good-looking sister had bought the drink and furthermore she wanted to know would I like to go out with her that same evening. Well, this was all very unexpected but, as I explained to Eddie, my ferry was leaving within the hour and I had to be on it. Because I was going back to Ireland. For good. He asked me to stay the night, but I said I couldn't possibly. When I was almost finished the second pint he asked me to stay again and this time I thought, 'Ah sure why not'. I'm sure it wasn't the first time that Guinness had come between a man and his ambition, and it certainly wouldn't be the last.

His sister grabbed a few minutes from the bar to sit with us and seemed delighted when I told her I'd stay. She asked me would I like to go to a nightclub when she finished work. I would indeed. By the time I should have been boarding the ferry Eddie was leading me to the living quarters upstairs, on his sister's instructions, to give me some dinner. I hadn't eaten in two and a half days and was delighted to see a big pot of stew cooking away on the stove. When I was finished the girl, Berny, appeared and told me that she would be ready to leave within an hour or so. There was just something about her. She didn't make me feel shy or self-conscious. It was a little peculiar to be sitting in a stranger's front room, but she soon put me at my ease. I couldn't take my eyes off her and I felt myself opening up to her in a way that I had never done before.

She brought me to a nightclub called Pandora's and we had a great night. At some point I began to feel that something bigger than me was taking place, and it was all to do with this ginger-haired girl. It was the strangest feeling. The easiest way to describe it is to say that somehow I knew, I just knew, that this girl was going to become my present, my future, my world. On the way back from the club she told me apologetically that I'd have to sleep in the bar as there was no room upstairs. On reaching the pub we sat up together for a few more hours and I told her a little bit about my life to date, a little bit about Olive, Patsy, Ken and St Patrick's. I didn't tell her everything, but I told her enough. She listened quietly and then asked to see my ticket for the ferry. When I handed it to her she tore it into little pieces and told me what I may have already guessed by then, that I wasn't going back to Ireland. She also told me that she would arrange for me to stay at the pub.

I woke up in the pool room of the pub the next morning at 7 am, taking a few minutes to remember where on earth I was. Oh yes, I wasn't in Cork, I was in Wales. I decided to venture outside and explore Swansea. The sun was climbing the sky and it looked like it was going to be another beautiful day. I felt a growing excitement as I walked around the area. I wasn't in Ireland, but I had this feeling that I had come home at last. There were lots of new buildings going up and when I found myself standing in front of a large building site called Debenhams, in the centre of Swansea, I plucked up the courage to march in and ask for the gaffer. Colin Mann, from Bonymaen, came out to meet me and I asked him for a job, and he gave me one. Just like that. He brought me around to introduce me to all his boys and kept me laughing all the way. I started there and then. At 10 am we filed into the canteen. I looked about awkwardly as I was still flat broke although there was nothing wrong with my appetite. Colin noticed immediately and asked had I any money. He paid my canteen bill until my first wages came through the following week.

After work I headed back to the Burrows Arms, much to the relief of the barmaid who, I was told, had spent the entire day looking for me. I must admit that this thrilled me. Her face lit up when she saw me and when I told her about my job she was delighted. She informed me that I was just in time for dinner. But first I was to come upstairs and meet her parents because I was moving in. But I was a mess, covered in clay and dust and in no fit state for company. She told me not to worry and handed me a couple of bags. She had spent her wages on clothes and shoes for me. All I could do was stare wordlessly at her. I followed her upstairs where I showered, shaved and changed into the new clothes. I felt transformed, but still quite unsteady at the idea of coming out to face her entire family at the dinner table. I could hear their voices from the safety of the bathroom but felt quite unable to go outside to meet them. No doubt I gave that bathroom a thorough cleaning while I was trying to find my courage. Olive's training hadn't gone to waste. Finally I was able to come out and meet everyone. They all welcomed me with open arms and made me sit down. I was a little apprehensive about eating in front of them. Although I had come from a big family myself I had, needless to say, never been allowed to eat with them. However I soon began, in spite of myself, to relax and enjoy their company. We joked about three Patricks living under the one roof, me, Berny's father and her brother. Her mother Brenda was exactly the kind of mother I would have loved: warm, caring and supportive. Altogether Berny had three brothers, Eddie, Patrick and Val, and just one sister, Patricia.

As soon as dinner was over I was invited downstairs for a drink and the night turned into a great session. As the regulars packed in I was introduced to them and typically everyone insisted on buying me a drink. As I said it was only a small bar, but it somehow managed to stretch to hold the crowd of Irish and Welsh and could even accommodate them when they wanted to stand and sway to whatever was on the juke box. I got very drunk that night, not entirely my own fault, and joined in with the singing as if I was one of the regulars. Afterwards Berny and I went for a walk down to the Bay. Thanks to the drink I was feeling very brave and asked her to be my girlfriend. She agreed. It was after four in the morning and we sat on the rocks, watching the tide roll in as the sun began to peep out above the horizon. I thought to myself that Heaven couldn't be too far from this. The search was over. Twenty years of struggle had finally paid off and now I was holding hands with this wonderful girl who looked at me as if I was someone truly special. In just twenty-four hours she had given me a roof over my head, a new wardrobe and a home. I experienced a fleeting moment of utter panic as I wondered how I could possibly repay her for all of this, whether I was even worth all of this, but I pushed it aside as we held hands and wondered how far it was to Cork city. She asked me again about my childhood, and cried freely at some of my answers. I fell in love that night, for the very first time.

Six weeks later I asked her to marry me and we got engaged. Two weeks later we admitted that we wanted to get married sooner rather than later and set the date for six weeks time. We invited my parents to come over. I hadn't stopped wanting a normal family life and watching how well my in-laws-to-be got on together – well, it had got me thinking again. It had been a couple of years since I saw Patsy and Olive, maybe things would be different now that I was a grown man with a wife. Also Berny encouraged me to contact them. Our wedding day just might prove to be a brand new beginning for all of us. And they came. Patsy, Olive and two of my sisters got the ferry across and stayed in the pub thanks to my mother-in-law farming her own family out to neighbours and relatives. They got the latest ferry crossing possible, getting into Swansea at 4 am, the morning of the wedding. Patsy immediately called me aside and asked where they were going to sleep. When I told him that they were being put up at the pub by Berny's mother he seemed far from happy. Olive looked completely ill at ease as she presented Berny and me with a toaster and two pillows. There was a general awkwardness all round with my family making absolutely no attempt to ingratiate themselves with Berny's. Fortunately though, it was late so we all just headed to bed.

The wedding service was seven hours later, at St David's Church in Swansea. Everything went perfectly. I was so proud of my gorgeous, young wife and couldn't stop smiling at her, at the priest, at the guests. When the service was over we were immediately surrounded by all our friends and Berny's family who threw confetti and hugged us in delight. As soon as I got the chance I looked around for my family, wanting to share my wealth of happiness with them. But I couldn't see them anywhere. That's odd I thought. Maybe they felt a bit shy in the crowd of strangers and headed back to the Burrows Arms, where we were having our reception, to wait for us there. About an hour later I realised that they were gone. Later I heard they took off after the service for a ten-day holiday in Nottingham. They never even said goodbye, never mind congratulating me or welcoming Berny into the family. Later again I discovered a possible reason for their sudden and discreet disappearance; a bag of money had gone missing from under the counter of the bar, along with a ring belonging to my father-in-law.

So now we were married and living happily above the pub with my in-laws. They were all the family I needed and thanks to them I discovered the joys of family get-togethers and the fun in celebrating Christmas, New Year, Easter, St Patrick's Day and birthdays. I was beginning my life anew, full of hope and possibility about the future, a life built on love instead of hate. It made sense to stay above the pub as I was away a lot with work. The construction business was busy enough and I often found myself working on sites miles away from Swansea. Nevertheless I enjoyed the work and the men I worked with, and because I had a proper family to come home to it actually made it easier to go away. Life was good, more than good. In fact it was great. I was happier than I had ever been.

But then, about six months after I got married, I went a bit mad.

# 'Mad Irishman'

I succumbed, body and soul, to the demon drink as if I had a special vocation for it – which I suppose I did in a way. I drank as if there was no present, no tomorrow. I drank as if there was only my past. Of course living above a busy, friendly bar did not help and when I thought I had gotten ridiculously drunk one too many times at the Burrows Arms I took myself off to another bar for a while and then onto another one. Pretty soon I was on first-name terms with every publican in Swansea. My wife used to wonder how I knew so many people. I even had my own nick-name with the locals; they called me the 'Mad Irishman'. I drank frequently and always with the intention of getting drunk to the point where I hardly knew my own name. It got so that I was spending hundreds of pounds a week on drink. I kept working so that I would have the money to buy alcohol. When I ran out of money I was quite capable of taking things from the house to sell them: the tumble dryer, jewellery, the television and the video recorder. I think the worst thing I ever did was to steal Berny's precious fur coat and sell it to buy booze.

A typical day included my bringing six to eight cans of cider to work with me. After a while I needed to bring an additional flask of rum or whiskey as the cider, from overuse, lost its ability to keep my memories properly at bay. When I knocked off work at 5 pm I headed straight to the pub where I would easily put away twelve pints of Guinness accompanied by twelve chasers of whisky. Only then was I drunk enough. One morning I woke up to find myself on a ferry which had just docked at Ireland. It took me ages to work out where I was and when I finally managed to recognise the innards of the ferry I looked out a porthole to see the sign, 'Welcome to Ireland'. Then, under the guise of 'Mad Irishman', I began my own little crime wave: drunken disorderliness, burglary and assaulting the police officers who came to save me from myself. It was only a matter of time before I ended up behind bars. I soon found myself in Swansea jail for twelve weeks until I got bail.

If this was a novel, you would probably be reading at this point about my moment of glorious epiphany while I sat in my cell reflecting on my actions, followed by the consequential complete transformation as I realised how much I loved my wife and so forth. And yes I did have plenty of time to ask myself what the hell was going on with me. I knew I was breaking Berny's heart and that I needed to get a grip, to take control of the situation – I just wasn't sure how I was to go about regaining control again. When I wasn't off my head I was mortified on discovering what I had done the night before. I wasn't drinking to be funny or entertaining, I was drinking to numb the pain that I naively thought my new life had banished. It shocked me to realise that the pain of my childhood and the thousands upon thousands of painful memories were still there, waiting to be faced. The shock vibrated through my entire being, making me doubt the foundations of my new existence, my new happiness. In short, it made me doubt myself.

I left jail with every intention of going straight. My day in court saw me fined, ordered to carry out community work and put on probation. I was so ashamed of myself and I swore that this was it. No more. I made elaborate promises, promises that I truly meant, to Berny, her family and my friends. Promises that I couldn't possibly keep. As it turned out I was only just getting started. That stint in Swansea jail was the beginning of seven long years of drunkenness, when I spent almost every weekend sleeping the drink off in a cell. On the plus side I managed to stop stealing and assaulting the cops who got to know me very well. Actually we developed quite a good relationship over the coming years. Every night I was out on a bender they would pull up beside me in the van, calling out to me:

'C'mon Paddy, jump in.'

And off we'd go back to the station where I looked forward to getting my head down. Then next morning, miserable in my hangover, the desk sergeant would joke,

'Ach Paddy! Not you again. Now tell me this, do you remember what you got up to last night?'

But I never could. I made sure of that.

'I know what we should do with you; how about we deport you back to the Emerald Isle? Ah I'm only joking with you.

Sure I'd miss seeing you if you were gone.'

With a pounding head and lurching belly I willed him to forget the banter and just get on with the business of charging me so that I could leave and return to the pub for a swift 'hair of the dog' or else I wouldn't be able to work. As I turned to go out the door several of the officers would call after me,

'Probably see you later tonight, Paddy?'

And they were usually right.

# My Own Family

In June of 1979 Berny told me she was pregnant. I couldn't believe it. I was going to be a father. Me. We clung to one another in delight and started making plans for our child's arrival and future. I decided it was high time we had our own place and went down to Swansea City Council to apply for a home. A few weeks later I was given a flat in Blaen-y-maes. Before Berny moved in I decorated the place myself because I wanted it to be perfect for her. She had put up with a lot over the last few months and had never once wavered in her love or support for me. I admired her strength and her steady belief in her unreliable husband. She alone knew what was driving me to drink like I did. Everyone else just thought I was an alcoholic who loved the taste of the hard stuff.

After the initial jubilation wore off bitter memories started to surface once more; in particular the images of Ken and me being dragged around by our penises as our demented mother roared at us, over and over again, that we would never be able to have children. A tense chill settled around my heart, keeping me awake at night. What if she's right? I accompanied Berny to all of her hospital appointments as if my very presence could ward off any potential mishaps. As I watched her get bigger and bigger I couldn't shake off the feeling that something was going to go wrong, that we were going to lose the baby. That maybe Olive had cursed me and now I had cursed Berny. The nine months crawled by. The day before she was due I was working in west Wales and didn't get back to the flat until late. I got a bad fright when I discovered that the flat was empty. I rang the Burrows to be told that Berny had gone into labour seven hours earlier and had been rushed to hospital.

When I got to the ward she was still in labour. I've never felt so useless in all my life. There was absolutely nothing I could do except sit and wait. Sometime after 2 am a doctor came out to see me, to tell me that he was very sorry, but my wife had given birth to a stillborn boy. I sank into the chair, all my fears realised. Olive's shade had followed me into this labour ward, having declared, many years ago, that this child of mine should not live. The doctor interrupted my self-recriminations to ask me if I wanted to see Berny just for a few minutes as she was in desperate need of sleep. In my blind despair I had completely forgotten about her. I held my wife for as long as I could and she cried like I never heard her cry before or since. Both of us were unaware, for the moment, of exactly how much guilt the other was carrying.

When I left the ward, after promising Berny that I would be back first thing in the morning, I noticed a phone box. I don't know why but I suddenly wanted to ring Tullamore and tell them what had happened. As I say I really don't know why, even to this day, I wanted to share my grief with them. As usual I hadn't a penny on me so I rang via an operator telling her to reverse the charges, and to tell whoever answered the phone that the call concerned the death of Patrick's son. I felt my face crumple up as I said the last two words. Less than two minutes later the operator asked me was I still there. I said yes, noticing that she sounded a bit strange.

'I apologise sir for this message, but this is the exact answer I got: "I don't care about him or his baby and don't phone here again."'

We eventually broke the spell, Berny and me. About twelve months later we had a daughter whom we named Michelle, followed by Mary Ann the following year. Fourteen months later, we welcomed Kathleen into the world, who was joined a year later by Sandra, and then by Patrick the year after that. Thirteen months after Patrick, James was born, and lastly – but by no means least – Sean.

# Home for the Holidays

In 1980 I decided to bring Berny to Tullamore as she had never been in Ireland before; she had also yet to meet some members of the Doyle family. I thought it would be a nice break for the two of us after the recent devastation of our lost baby. Because we were on a tight budget we had to plan weeks ahead of the trip and I contacted Patsy and Olive to let them know we'd be coming to stay with them for a weekend. Their acceptance led to an avalanche of letters filled with little requests. Patsy wanted some car parts, a decoder box for his satellite equipment while Olive wanted dresses. The letters got more frequent as our holiday date neared and I developed a nagging anxiety about the fact that not once did the writer tell us that they were looking forward to seeing us. It was turning into an expensive trip and this was even before we started packing our suitcases. I knew that I'd have to bring good presents on top of the specifically requested gifts to ensure that our visit went smoothly.

That nagging anxious feeling turned into full-blown

misgivings by the time we boarded the train in Dublin. What was I doing bringing Berny to Tullamore? She was such a good, kind-hearted girl, who only wanted to think the best of everyone. Surely I knew that this could only be bloody horrible for the both of us? Naturally I kept all this from my smiling wife; I was frankly touched by her genuine excitement at seeing where I grew up and I also wanted to show her off. She was my good luck talisman, representing how far I had come from robbing stale food out of the neighbours' bins. All I could do was hope for the best. When the train pulled into Tullamore I stifled an urge to stay where I was. My palms were actually sweating when I lifted our cases off the rack and climbed gingerly down onto that all too familiar platform. Memories of the scared, hungry boy that I had been almost toppled me back onto the steps of the train. I scanned the car park apprehensively, wondering if anyone had come to collect us. They hadn't; despite all of them living around the area and owning cars. I hid my disappointment from Berny and told her that she'd get a proper eyeful of the town as we walked through it to reach my parent's house which was about a mile away from the station.

We had quite a lot of luggage, which was mostly gifts for the family, so it was a bit of a trudge. To be honest I found it embarrassing to walk through town carrying my suitcases. On the other hand Berny beamed proudly when lots of people recognised me and called out, 'Welcome home, Patrick'. My heart shuddered on seeing the house. It had been a long, long time since I had stood in it. Gritting my teeth I rang the doorbell. True to form, when Olive opened the door her first words were not particularly welcoming,

'How long are you here for?'

She took some of the luggage into the sitting room while I was sorting out the rest of it. I had brought four hundred duty-free cigarettes to hand out as gifts, two cottage ornaments and a jacket for myself. The next morning was Sunday and I went into the sitting room to retrieve the duty-free bags but they were gone. I couldn't ask about them and risk Berny and me being told to leave the house so I didn't mention them when I went into the kitchen where Berny was sitting with my parents. Since it was almost 11.30 am I asked Berny if she wanted to go to noon mass. When she said yes I told Olive not to bother putting food on for us as we would go to a restaurant instead, explaining that I didn't want to put her out. But, much to my surprise, Olive told us to go to church and that she'd have the dinner ready when we came back. On the way to mass Berny told me that she was starving and very much looking forward to her Sunday roast.

Well, it wasn't to be and I don't know why I expected it to be otherwise. When we got back to the house Patsy and Olive were just finishing up their dinner. The oven was empty and I immediately knew that there was nothing left for us. Berny, however, joined them at the table, smiling innocently at the pair of them, telling them about the mass. Olive got up, put on the kettle and slowly reached into the biscuit tin. She put two plain biscuits on a saucer and handed them to my wife. With that I lost my head and started shouting, my usual dormant rage stirred up as I saw my lovely Berny being subjected to the typical treatment. I stormed upstairs to grab our suitcases while Olive took the opportunity to ask a now sobbing Berny had we argued while we were out.

It was a scorching hot day as I marched us back to the station, a mere eleven hours after we had arrived. I just wanted to get back to Wales as fast as possible. However the train to Dublin wasn't due for another eight hours. Of course, the Sunday timetable; that humourless invention that curtails too much travel or having too much fun on 'the day of rest'. We were both hungry and thirsty, but it was too far to walk to the shops with our big cases and Berny was too upset to let me go off and get us something. Plus I didn't want to bump into any of the family and neither did I want any of the people who greeted me yesterday to see me leaving so soon again. It was ridiculous. I cursed Olive to a height that day, as well as myself for my own stupidity.

I stayed away from Ireland for the next five years. Angry letters followed me across the Irish Sea to tell me to stay away for good. So I did. When I next visited Ireland I just hung out with friends, giving up on contacting my parents again. Nevertheless I had been seen about the town. Shortly after I got back to Wales I received a letter from Olive written in red ink which made me hang my head in shame.

*Your father has cried for the last three days. He heard you were home and you didn't even call in to see him. He's very hurt. After all he never did anything to you, it was me and you who didn't get on.*

# An Expensive Habit

About five years after I came off the drink I accidentally developed another expensive habit. It began innocently enough, as most of these habits do. A friend encouraged me to try some cannabis to see if it relaxed me. Unfortunately I found that not only did it relax me wonderfully, but I also really, really liked it. Pretty soon I was meeting other like-minded people and someone suggested that I try amphetamines. So I did and they made me feel like I was on top of the world. In quite a short amount of time my new amphetamine habit was costing me £40 a day, a great deal more expensive than ordinary cigarettes.

Gradually I replaced the amphetamines with a brand new kick called ecstasy. Now this drug introduced me to a whole new social life. I became a 'raver' much to my embarrassment today. My friends and I began travelling around to the different nightclubs throughout Swansea and Wales. It's a terrible cliché, but the 'buzz' was addictive, not only from the little tablets themselves, but also from the loud, pulsating, hyper music, the lights that flashed in time to your speeded-up heartbeat and the young people, hooked on fun, who took their dancing oh so very seriously. The lyrics of the songs, when there were lyrics, inspired the hip congregation to feel good and free in the moment by ridding our minds of trouble and strife. It was a sort of Heaven. The clubs were like a warm cocoon keeping me safe from my life outside. Everyone was so damned happy inside. Plus I got to be the teenager that I never was.

Of course, for every high there is a cascading low. The thrill of the ecstasy began to wane and I had to substitute it with something a bit more sombre, namely acid and then cocaine. I was sinking deeper and deeper. What used to be a £40 a day habit leapt into a whopping expenditure of £500 a week. At some point I was obliged to start selling drugs in order to meet the cost of my own habit. My weight plummeted as did my moods. The whole experience had begun with my trying cannabis in order to chill out and now I had to take that many different drugs, to maintain my happy feeling, that I was practically suicidal once more.

It was utterly, utterly mad. For four years I was deep in debt, financially and mentally. My marriage and entire domestic life were falling to pieces around me and I was too confused to work out what the hell I was supposed to do. It was a wheel of horror, taking drugs, selling drugs to make money to take drugs and so on, and on, and on. Friends of mine died from overdoses; others lived but only after destroying their families. One of my lowest points was when I found myself owing £6000 with only a short amount of time to pay it. Finally, somehow, I figured out what I had to do and I picked a significant date to put my plan into action. On New Year's Eve, 1999, while presumably everyone else was out partying to welcome either the end of the world or the new millennium, depending on their point of view, I locked myself into my bedroom to come off drugs all by myself. And I did it without any professional help. And no it wasn't easy at all. In fact it was downright bloody awful, but at least I knew there would be an end to it.

# Mental Cruelty

I travelled to Tullamore in 2002 for St Patrick's Day, a favourite day of mine, and I always tried to visit Ireland to celebrate it there. And it wasn't for the Guinness that I was making the trip, I had given up drinking about ten years earlier. As much as I love Swansea and Wales, and feel thoroughly at home there, my love for Ireland has always been constant, more than likely heightened by the fact that I am living elsewhere. One of my sisters had invited me to stay at her house; therefore there wasn't any quaking of my knees – or any other limbs – when I stepped down from the Dublin train on 16 March. To my great surprise my parents were waiting for me in the car park and not only that, but they were smiling and seemed really happy to see me. This was fantastic; I still hadn't given up on my dream of having normal parents and this sort of scenario was exactly what I envisaged as having 'normal relations' with them. I jumped into the back of the car and we had a great chat all the way back to the house.

I was told not to bother staying with any of my sisters or

brothers; sure they were all prostitutes and drug dealers. This was a normal conversation about their children and I was so used to it I didn't bother asking them what on earth they meant; I knew it was all completely untrue. When we reached the house I went through all my bags, sorting out what gifts were for whom. I had planned to get Patsy cigarettes on the ferry, completely unaware that there was no more duty free, it had been a while since I had made this journey. So he was the only person I hadn't got something for. I explained all of this to them, telling them that I would buy him cigarettes in the local shop. However Olive shook her head.

'Your father hasn't smoked in over a year, but he does need a new pair of shoes. We saw a lovely pair in town last week and they were only fifty quid.'

I didn't say a word. I only had eighty quid with me and I had promised my kids that I would bring them back presents. You might wonder why I didn't just tell my parents this, but that's the thing about being wholly dominated as a child. Sitting there in that house, in that kitchen, which had been the location for the some of the worst experiences of my life, I found it extremely difficult, especially when I was alone with them, to remember that I was now a grown man with my own family and responsibilities. Without realising it I automatically slipped back into the role of a tentative child trying to make his parents like him. So I just sat there, hoping that they would just forget about the shoes and we could talk about something else. After maybe ten minutes of the three of us staring into space Olive finally asked Patsy,

'Well, are you not going to get your shoes before they're sold out?'

Patsy sniffed and replied,

'I'm just waiting for my son to get his wallet out.'

They both looked at me and I crumbled. With a tightness in my chest I handed over my precious money and off he went to buy his shoes. At least friendly relations had been maintained. Surely that much was worth fifty quid.

Olive suggested I go into the lounge as she had to prepare dinner for my younger brother, my sister and her boyfriend. I was pretty hungry myself by now so I went inside to relax and wait. When the three arrived she had them sit down at the table, immediately serving up their meal to them. It smelled gorgeous. They had already started eating when I was called into the kitchen and asked if I wanted anything. She knew I would say no. And I honestly couldn't help myself. I was hungry, there was plenty of food and yet, and yet, at the grand old age of forty-two years and as a father of seven children myself, I heard myself trot out the answer I had learned to say for sixteen years,

'No thanks. I'm not hungry.'

She handed me a cup of tea and I sat there, chatting away, watching them eat their food. Starving. Like the good old days. As soon as they finished their meal she brought the bin in from the back garden and began scraping the substantial leftovers into it, while keeping her eyes on me the entire time.

When I got back to Berny I told her that I would never set

foot in that house again and that I didn't care if I never saw Patsy or Olive again.

✉ ✉ ✉

A few months later I received another letter from Olive telling me to send my father a card as his sixty-fifth birthday was approaching. I was earning good money then so I sent over a birthday card with £100 worth of postal orders, making sure I got a receipt of postage for such a valuable letter. Two weeks went by and I heard nothing. I decided to ring home. Patsy answered and I wished him a belated happy birthday, much to his surprise.

'Are you drunk? My birthday isn't for another five months.'

I asked him to put Olive on the phone, and then asked her had my card arrived. Of course she said 'no', but did tell me that she had only been pulling my leg about my father's birthday. On hearing that the card held £100 she began to advise me how to go about investigating its loss with the post office. I didn't know whether to believe her or not. A couple of years later one of my sisters told me that she had been in the house when the card arrived and my mother had laughed her head off. I realise now that she never actually asked me to put money into the card; that was my choice. But she is my mother and knows me only too well.

It seems to me that she has never stopped wanting to make a fool out of me. Our whole relationship has been a game to her, and I must be on the longest losing streak in history. It feels like I'm caught on some sort of treadmill. No matter what they've done to me, or what they continue to do to me, I always go back hoping it will be better this time. For instance why did I send over £100? I could have just sent a card like she asked me to. Was I showing off my relatively good wage? Was I trying to buy their affection, or their validation of my life?

✉ ✉ ✉

One summer about fifteen years ago, I was working at the Port Talbot Steel works, just outside Swansea. When I got home there were fifteen plates of salads sitting on the countertop in the kitchen. This was unexpected. As far as I knew it wasn't anyone's birthday, or my wedding anniversary. Also the house smelled strongly of polish and cleanser and was unusually tidy. In the living room I found the dining table completely kitted out with our good delph, napkins and candles. A highly excited Berny burst in the front door, with piles of shopping bags, telling me in a rush that she had spent the previous twelve hours scrubbing the house and had moved around all the bedrooms upstairs, even borrowing a bed from the lady who lived next door to us. She was just back from Tesco where she had gone to buy extra bedding. In answer to my wonderstruck face she giggled.

'You'll never guess what's happening!'

I told her my mind was a complete blank.

'Would you believe I got a phone call this morning to tell me that your whole family are coming over tonight? They rang from Fishguard Harbour and said that they hoped to be here about 8 pm.'

I was thrilled by the news. It had been more than five years since I had had any kind of contact with any of my family, and I suppose I still, against all odds, had not given up hope on maintaining, or indeed establishing, a normal working relationship with them. That they were coming to see my home and my family was more than I would ever have expected. I hugged Berny and went running upstairs to shower and dress since it was after 7.30 already. By 8 pm I was outside my backdoor, sitting on the step, enjoying the last bit of sun and waiting for the sound of a car in the driveway. The sun set a couple of hours later, but there was still no sign of them. I began to get worried. At 11 pm I was convinced that something terrible had happened so I rang the Ferry Port to see if there had been any accidents and was much relieved to hear there hadn't been. There was no point ringing Tullamore since the whole lot of them were in Wales. Thanks to my close connections with the local police I was able to ring the station and have them check whether there had been any car accidents on the road from Fishguard to Swansea. Again I was relieved to hear that no accidents had been reported. I thought maybe they had got delayed and didn't like to come to the house when it got so late. Therefore they may have booked into a hotel. It was the only plausible explanation, or else they were lost somewhere. I sent Berny and the disappointed kids to bed and stayed up all night by myself worrying. Like a fool. At some point between four and five in the morning I threw the limp salads in the bin. Finally at 9 am I rang the house in Tullamore, for the want of something better to do. Patsy answered. When he heard the confusion in my voice he laughed heartily.

'Did your wife tell you we had her going yesterday?'

I said that no, she did not tell me that, but she had made up their dinner and all the beds and we had sat here waiting for them all evening. He laughed even louder at this.

'Ha, Ha! We were just joking with her'

✉ ✉ ✉

My children call me the 'Cave Man' thanks to my peculiar eating habits. Living out of bins for the first sixteen years of my life has left its mark on me. I have little patience today when it comes to cooking, or even just heating up, food. I prefer to eat raw sausages, raw bacon and raw fish instead of waiting for them to turn brown under the grill or in a frying pan. The few minutes that it takes to heat up a can of soup, or beans, or peas are simply minutes I don't feel I have when I'm hungry. So I just eat everything cold; vegetables, meat, baked beans, mushy peas and basically anything else that comes in a tin. I eat onions like someone else eats apples. And I eat very fast, swallowing in gulps, almost as if I'm afraid my wife or one of the kids will wink at me to lay down whatever I have in my hands and pretend to the world that I'm not hungry.

# The Last Straw

There was a knock at our door one morning, about 4 am to be precise, and when I finally got the door opened I found myself face to face with Patsy, of all people. I thought he was still in America and in any case I certainly wasn't used to receiving visits from him. He had a small suitcase with him and a large steel box on two wheels. While Berny put on the kettle he explained that he had just gotten back from the States and Olive told him to come to Swansea so that I could get him a job. I stared at him in amazement and told him that I was actually unemployed, and had been for a while. It was the early 1990s and there wasn't much work around. He replied that he was virtually penniless, that he had run out of work in America and was now desperate to make some money. We had no money to lend him, when he asked, so I had Berny ask her mother for a loan of £300, which Patsy promised to pay back as soon as he could.

He wanted to buy a car and said that with some wheels under us we would be able to set ourselves up as house renovators; we could travel to wherever the work took us. It sounded like a good idea. With seven young children in the house my dole money was hardly lasting from week to week. Also I knew that Patsy was good at his job so there would be no trouble getting work, once word got out. There was an advertisement in the paper that night for a £190 car. We rang the owner immediately and went around to see it, deciding to buy it there and then. The next morning Patsy walked over to our local post office to send Olive £100 of the £300 loan from my mother-in-law. He then took the car for a practice run around the estate and when he got back he complained that the car needed new brake pads. I had no money until the Family Allowance came through and told him this, sending him into a sulk.

Berny got the Allowance on Monday morning and with some misgivings, on both our parts, gave me and Patsy half of the money to fix up the car. For the next seven weeks he stayed in our house. My dole and the Children's Allowance now had to feed seven children and three adults. Since Patsy was a smoker we also had to buy him a box of twenty every single day. He also got more money out of us for the car, every few days telling us that it needed something else. It seemed to me that he was just using us to rebuild a brand new car and had no intention of setting us up in business. It was a crazy situation and I reacted to the burgeoning stress in my usual way at this time; I went out and spent precious money on getting plastered. When I came home drunk Berny told me that it looked like we were all moving to Ireland. I couldn't understand what she was saying, but seemingly I had to talk to Patsy about it.

When I got up the next morning I found my father and Berny in the kitchen. He asked me if I was sober and when I nodded my aching head he told me that it was all sorted. I got myself a cup of tea while he told me that Olive wanted us all to come back and live in Tullamore. Looking at Berny's worried face I asked him where we would live, that I had no money to buy a house.

'Your grandmother's house is empty now, you could live there. It's a grand sized house for the kids and I'd help you do it up. Sure what have you got to lose? You can't get work here, you said so yourself.'

I felt very confused. My granny's house was a lovely house alright, but moving back to Tullamore? Uprooting Berny and the kids? On the other hand I needed to get back to work. Maybe Patsy and I could make a go of it in Ireland, even just for a few years.

Patsy must have given it a lot of thought as he had it all worked out. Berny and I just needed to sell off the big furniture and we could fill the car with what we needed to bring over to the old house, and take the ferry back together. We were being railroaded into agreeing to the move. Doubts were pricking away at my brain, but I didn't voice them. I know I should have, but Patsy was a very persuasive man. He made it sound so attractive, living in the bosom of the Doyles again. There was the fact that most of my brothers and sisters were living around the area, with their own families, and I couldn't help thinking that it would be nice for my kids to meet their

Irish cousins. Berny watched me go through the different emotions until it was settled. Her unfailing loyalty allowed her to support me in whatever I chose to do. I wasn't even sure that I supported myself, or if I had even made a proper decision, but before I knew it Patsy was cheerfully boxing up our belongings, stretching duct tape around the edges of cardboard boxes given to him by our local supermarket.

Berny went around the neighbours selling off the big stuff like the beds, the wardrobes, the fridge, the carpets and the suite of furniture. She made £800 in total, £300 of which we gave to Patsy; although I can't remember why. A couple of days later, far from happy, but unable to call a halt to the proceedings, I led my wife and seven children on to the ferry. We were taking the Swansea to Cork route as it was the only one available. Patsy drove the car onboard and we all met up in the TV room. My nerves started to chatter and a few minutes after the boat pushed off from Swansea I left everyone to go to the bar where I got well and truly hammered. I'm not proud of my behaviour. I felt the whole thing was a mistake and beyond my control, so that drinking myself into an obstreperous frame of mind was the only pro-active option available to me. When it appeared obvious that I had had way too much to drink the barman naturally refused to serve me, and that's when I lost my head. There was a dreadful row; I was shouting my head off at the captain, who was called to deal with me, and at his staff who were trying bravely to calm me down. After a bit of a struggle I insisted on getting back to my family. About five or six deckhands followed me, wanting to bring me downstairs, away from the other passengers, but I wasn't having any of it. When I reached the TV room Patsy quickly realised what was up and told the crew to leave me be, that I was his son and he'd make sure I didn't cause any more trouble – which was probably the nicest thing he has ever done for me. Flopping miserably into a chair I closed my eyes and fell asleep until we reached Cork and it was time to disembark. Berny woke me up and made me drink a lot of tea to clear my head a bit. And it worked. My head was so clear that I was able to watch my father drive the car – which was full of our bedding, curtains, cutlery, pots, pans, towels, toys, complete collection of family photos, Christmas decorations, camera, and video recorder – right through customs, past the space where I presumed he would stop to wait for us and off into the distance. In a few short minutes he was gone from my sight. Perhaps the longest walk of my life was the few hundred steps I took to my wife, who was waiting for me with the children, to tell her that Patsy and all our stuff was gone.

It took us four long, depressing months to get back to Swansea. We took the coach from Cork harbour to the bus station and there I rang a mate of mine, explaining what had happened. He took us back to his mother's house, trying to get me to ring the police on my father. But I couldn't do it. Nobody had enough room for our family so we were obliged to split up amongst the houses of my friend's kindly relatives. Five weeks later we finally got a house from Cork council, an unfurnished, three bed-roomed house in Mayfield. I rang Olive out of desperation and asked her could I at least have the blankets and curtains back.

'No. Patsy threw them out because they weren't any use to us.'

'What do you mean? Those curtains were only new.'

'Well, we didn't need any curtains since we have blinds on the windows now.'

And then she hung up on me.

I had to go to the local priest and beg for help with buying furniture and fittings. Berny cried every day until we were able to go back to Wales. When we got back there was a letter waiting for me in the Burrows Arms. Inside I found two photographs. One of the photos was of our blue curtains sitting on what I knew to be the carpet of Olive's sitting room. Someone had written on the back, 'Your curtains'. The second photo was of the car that Patsy had bought with my mother-in-law's loan, the one that Berny and I had paid to have virtually rebuilt. In the photo the car was parked in Patsy's garage, and on the back, in the same handwriting, was the caption 'My car'. I still have those photos today.

# No Escape

Most people leave their childish fears behind when they become adults. I can't, and neither can Ken. For one thing there was nothing childish about our fear of Olive. As she battered, whipped and cut us she would tell us that she was going to beat us to death. Considering our circumstances, we had no reason not to believe her. For years, I was told I was ugly, I deserved to die, and I was a devil. Many a time I was forced to try and grab fistfuls of water out of our toilet, half-crazed after three days without food or liquid. She hated me. It was as simple as that. My mother absolutely and utterly loathed me, the very sight of me, maybe from the moment I was placed in her arms after birth. I've spent a lifetime wondering why and trying to reverse her hatred to love. I'm a grandfather now, several times over, and I still can't understand how someone actively hates a baby. Ken and I have spent many, many hours in the last few years trying to find the answer to that question. We find ourselves wondering again and again why she didn't just send us out to be adopted. She hated us, and still does, I'm sure.

It's Easter Sunday morning. I'm writing this in my mother-in-law's caravan in South Wales. I can hear excited children running around outside showing off their Easter eggs. Such a simple scene as this plunges me back into that murky past when I had to steal all the eggs for my younger brothers and sisters, except Ken. I dreaded Easter, even before Patsy went away to America. It was always the same. All us kids were rounded up in the kitchen to receive our eggs from our father. Olive would have already warned me only to eat a tiny piece of the egg that Patsy was about to give me. When he asked what was wrong, I was to tell him that I didn't want any more because I felt sick.

'I worked hard to buy these eggs and now you feel sick after just one bloody bite?' Obviously Patsy was under the impression that his wife had bought the eggs with the housekeeping money he gave her.

My mother would make a big fuss and tell him to share my egg out between the others. He'd call me an ungrateful bastard and send me to my room. As I headed for the stairs I'd hear her say,

'There! I told you he's never happy unless he's causing a row.'

Afterwards she would creep up to tell me that I was going to pay for the tiny piece of egg that she had told me to eat.

The reality of that hatred is with me every day of my life. The nightmares are still with me over forty years later. She used to tell the two of us that she would haunt us for the rest of our lives and by Jesus she was right. I'm in therapy now, doing my best to confront the shadow she has cast over my life.

Thanks to her I was in and out of prison for years. Thanks to her I almost drank myself into the gutter. When I walk around my own home in Swansea I constantly see my mother out of the corner of my eye. Every night I wake up sweating in the belief that she's standing at the end of my bed, ready to drag me out by the hair to do some ridiculous mammoth household task. My body is covered in scars from the beatings and I have had a lot of problems with my spine from the constant marathon thrashings. I'm told that I suffer from Post-Traumatic Stress and I have to take tablets to help with the frightening flashbacks.

On 24 August 2002 the phone rang at about 4 am. It was my kid brother Ken, who I hadn't seen or spoken to in about twenty years. Whenever I asked for any news of him on my visits to Tullamore I was always told he was in jail in America, but nobody ever seemed to remember which jail exactly. There never seemed to be an up-to-date address for him. I understand now that it was probably in Olive's best interest to keep us apart. Ken sounded agitated and upset as he began to tell me the strangest story I had ever heard – about two boys who were hated so much by their mother that she starved them and beat them to within an inch of their lives. But the strangest part of the story was that everyone, unbeknown to the two children – who typically didn't want to get their mother into trouble and, therefore, never breathed a word about her behaviour to teachers, priests, doctors, policemen or social workers – knew what was going on.

# Part Three:

# Ken

1969 TWO OF THREE

**NOTES**

REGISTER NO. .................. FRIEND'S ADDRESS ..................

(2)

31. XII. 69.
Vomited once tonight
Father says that child is neglected – only getting one meal / day

O/E T° 101.5°F P. 120/min
Child emaciated – not dehydrated
Quite an intelligent little boy.
Abdomen: [illegible] Tongue moist
[illegible] bowels [illegible]
pot-belly
No [illegible] Chest clear No cough or chest colds
DIET ... [illegible] ... No glands [illegible]
[illegible]

| DATE | TREATMENT (Including Extra Diet and Stimulants) | DATE | TREATMENT (Including Extra Diet and Stimulants) |
|---|---|---|---|
| | Rx Food ++ | | |
| | Vitamins | | |
| | [illegible] | | |
| | 1. Weight → 27½ lb | | |
| | 2. X-Ray: Chest | | |
| 5/1/70 | [illegible] toes [illegible] side | | |
| | are infected – blistering. | | |
| | [illegible] | | |
| [illegible]/1/70 | [illegible] | | |
| | [illegible] | | |
| [illegible] | next clinic | | |

FILM DATE please

(B)

# Running From the Past

*'This boy is at risk within the family environment and I am very concerned that something be done for him.'*
(Social Worker's Report, 19 March 1976)

The only woman I've ever been attracted to is the singer Debbie Harry, from the American group Blondie. My life – or perhaps it would be more accurate to call it my existence – today is affected in a number of different ways by my brutal childhood and this is just one of them. My mother put me off women for good. I've never been in a relationship because I'm much too angry most of the time. When I'm not angry, I'm depressed and when I'm not depressed, I'm distraught over the loss of my life. As far as I am concerned Olive wasn't really a woman, she was a monster. Throughout my childhood I spent a lot of time wondering how my father could stay married to her. I don't believe in love, or maybe I don't believe that someone can love me unconditionally, and I certainly don't have any faith that I can love another human being properly. On the other hand I could probably hate a person very well indeed.

I'm still running from the past that has followed me across the Atlantic Ocean to the United States of America where I've lived for the last twenty-three years. A day of ease simply does not exist for me. Instead, the ghostly but devastating threads of emotional and physical abuse trip me up several times in the morning, in the afternoon, in the evening and, in particular, during the long, dark night when I can't sleep; or if I do, it's only to find myself submerged in a nightmarish world, where I'm back in that bleak house in Tullamore. Certainly the pain is with me every day. Olive's beatings have permanently damaged my spine. The pain prevents me from working and also triggers the flashbacks; the memories of those scenes that are the source of my problems today. When I was nine years old I ended up in traction, in Tullamore hospital, for sixteen weeks, after my mother broke my leg. While we waited for the ambulance she bribed me with chocolate, and her fear, to tell the doctors that I had fallen down the stairs all by myself. Because hospitals did not have such a thing as a MRI machine then, the initial damage to my lower spine could not be detected. Olive told me that if I told everyone what really happened she would be locked up and I'd never see her again. Her fate was in my hands and I was much impressed with the weight of the responsibility. She needed me. As it happens the doctor would not believe my story, but he couldn't prove his suspicions.

'Ken, I know you didn't fall down the stairs. Someone did this to you. Now don't be afraid. I just want you to tell me the truth.'

'I fell down the stairs!'

My mother was always true to her word. While she was beating us she constantly told us that she would cripple us, haunt us, and kill us. There have been many times when I felt she did in fact carry out that last threat.

I rarely sleep the whole night through. And perhaps this is another thing that has prevented me from *ever* even attempting to pursue a relationship with a woman. There are the nights when I wake up crying, mentally crawling on my hands and knees out from under the dark veil of a nightmare. There is little variation in my dreams. They always include Olive in the starring role – and they always, *always* frighten me to the point of tears. I realise that this may be a little hard to appreciate if you have had a relatively normal childhood. But think about it for a minute. When my entire personality was being developed, my body, my intellect, my sense of the world, it was in an atmosphere of unrelenting dread. I dreaded getting up in the morning, I dreaded the pain and distress of my constant hunger, and I dreaded being hurt. This went on for years. I was only eighteen months old, a toddler, when I was first physically attacked by my mother and it soon became a way of life. That level and length of abuse, or at least my feelings regarding it, is a very hard thing to shake off.

On a more practical level the years of starvation, of never knowing when I might get to eat again, have left me with a very ambiguous relationship with food. If the nightmares don't wake me up then my still-anxious belly does. I regularly raid my own kitchen in the middle of the night and have no memory of doing it until I open my eyes the next morning and find the evidence strewn about my room. Like most Irish men I enjoy bacon and sausages; unlike most Irish men I eat mine raw, because that is how I ate them for years. There was no one or no time to fry or grill them, especially if I had plucked them out of someone's bin. To this day I cannot sit down and eat a meal with a group of people. I cannot bear the feeling that someone is watching me eat, a throwback to when Olive would deign to give me one spoonful of tea, in a mug, and a tiny square piece of dry bread, on a dinner plate, which I had to carefully dissect, using both a knife and fork and chew copiously before swallowing. And she never took her eyes off me as I pretended to feast on the same dinner that had been handed out simultaneously to my brothers and sisters.

About twenty years ago I was sitting in a restaurant in the Bronx, New York, reading my paper and minding my own business. The restaurant was a popular place for Irish ex-pats winding down after a hard day's work. This guy who looked about my age approached the table.

'Excuse me, but I have to ask. Are you by any chance a Doyle from Tullamore?'

'Yes, I'm Kenneth Doyle, though most people call me Ken.'

'Aha! I do know you!! You used to steal my lunch at school!'

He was a friendly guy who readily laughed at the memory of his disappearing lunches, but I couldn't share his sense of humour. Stealing food from other kids was an absolute necessity; however it never sat easy with me. As my old school friend and I talked about the past I wished for the ground to open up and swallow me. Patrick and I were expelled from one school after another for stealing food. Surely somebody, a teacher or a school principal, wondered why the same two children, from the same family, would be driven to rob, over and over again, another child's lunch. Each school relationship ended the same way, with plenty of visits to the head office and questions as to why we had stolen something. The emphasis was always on the action and never on what we had actually taken. Perhaps if all our teachers had focused on the product in question, food, more useful questions might have been asked. We didn't want to tell the truth, but we would dearly have loved for someone to guess it without our help.

Olive has also affected my financial situation. For one thing I can't afford the operation to fix my spine. An estimate from the pain management centre that I attend has put the cost of the surgery required as being somewhere in the region of $500,000. For the last six years I have been paying $600 a month for my pain killers and medications. I wrote to Brian Cowen, my fellow Offaly man, who was then the Minister for Finance. He made some enquiries for me and let me know what my entitlements were. Payment for the cost of my counselling is arranged through the Irish government, but the funding covers counselling only, and does not cover the medication my counsellor says I need to take.

Every two weeks, for the last seven years, without fail, I

see my psychologist who always seems very relieved that I haven't committed suicide since our previous session. I refuse to make any promises on this subject. The intention to kill myself has been with me for a very long time now. When I was about eleven years old I decided that I'd rather take my own life than continue surviving under Olive's roof. She had just beaten me senseless for something, for anything really, and I made my decision after I was locked into the bedroom. It had been a couple of days since I last ate and all things considered I was ready to give up. I hurriedly wrote out my brief suicide note which I left in place for my brother Michael who couldn't fail to see it when he came to bed. It went something along the lines of,

*To whom it may concern,*

*Ken Doyle was starved for two days and so decided to kill himself here.*

The first obstacle to carrying out my plan was my lack of preparation. It was only when I had fished out my school tie and started to look about the torture chamber, our bedroom, that I realised there was nowhere decent to hang myself from. I was stumped until I hit upon the idea of throwing myself out the window. However there was another obstacle to this second plan; Olive herself. When I pulled back the curtains I saw that she was in the yard and I had to quickly retreat since neither Patrick nor I were allowed to look out the windows. Had she seen me peeking out that day I would have received another hiding for my audacity.

Sometimes it seemed that she beat me out of pure boredom. There was a large closet at the top of the stairs, full to the brim with all my brothers' and sisters' clothes. It became the focal point for a sort of tortuous game that involved only the two of us. She would roar my name and I'd run to her to find her standing in front of the closet which was now completely emptied out. The contents had been kicked down the stairs as far as they would fall. The first time this happened I was bewildered, thinking there had been some sort of earthquake or equally devastating accident. But no, it was only my mother wanting to have her bit of fun with me. Standing there, breathing heavily, with the 'Cheese Please!' board in her hand she would address me loudly, grandly.

'Now Celli, you have fifteen minutes to put everything back in its right place or else I'll beat the living daylights out of you.'

It was an impossible job. For one thing there were far too many items to retrieve in such a small amount of time and for another thing I was much too small to reach to the high shelves – and God forbid that I'd ask for a chair or a stool. Nevertheless I never stopped trying to complete the task even though I knew in my heart that a beating was inevitable. She didn't want me to succeed with her request; what she wanted was to beat the living daylights out of me. That's all.

✉ ✉ ✉

I was a terrible crybaby when I was a child. I think it took me a long time to get used to the treatment that was meted out to Patrick and myself. Certainly for the first eight or nine years of my life I shed some amount of tears. I cried from the constant ache of hunger, I cried out of pure fear of Olive, I cried for hours after a beating. I had pains in my legs, my arms and my back. At school I absentmindedly felt the lumps and bumps on my body as I struggled to concentrate on my lessons. For those first few years I never gave up hoping that she'd change, that I'd wake up one day and she'd love me like the other mothers in the town loved their sons. At 2.30 pm I'd watch my friends being collected by their smiling mothers. It fascinated me how the mothers would look delighted to see their little girls and boys, some of them actually opened up their arms to let their kids run into a hug.

When she saw me upset it grated terribly on her,

'Celli if you don't take that dying face off you I will cut it off with a knife!'

✉ ✉ ✉

When I was about eleven years of age Patsy came home from America and decided to take his family on a holiday to County Mayo. We rented a cottage from a local family in the small, picturesque village of Louisburgh. Our nearest shop was about a mile away, it was a small shop, attached to a house, which sold all different kinds of things and had its own post office. Olive told me to go to the shop and see what I could get. As usual she gave me the money to buy something, maybe washing powder, telling me to bring the money back to her.

I walked the mile to the shop and was very relieved upon entering to find it empty. Perhaps the owner was having a cup of tea in his kitchen. Thank goodness there were no security cameras in those days. I leapt over the counter and opened a normal looking drawer to find it full of money; presumably this drawer was an informal cash register. It was a wonderful surprise. I grabbed a wad of £20 notes and shoved them down my trousers. As I climbed back over the counter, I accidentally kicked the drawer, sending all its heavy coins to the floor. The noise was terrific. I tore out the door and was about to start sprinting for my life when a man, presumably the owner, came running out in a panic, begging me to hold on for a minute. I thought I was surely done for. Imagine my amazement when he only wanted to know had I seen anyone in his shop. Giddy with gratitude I was at pains to be as much help as I could to the stricken shopkeeper. So I told him I had just seen a man cycle down the road at great speed, almost like he had done something wrong and was trying to get away as fast as possible. The poor guy thanked me, jumped into his car and flew off to give chase to a phantom cyclist. Meanwhile the real thief ran all the way back to the cottage, the £20 notes crunching with every step. There was a few hundred pounds in my pants that day which made my mother very happy. As a result I had a very good holiday.

# St Joseph's

At twelve years of age my parents drove me down to Galway. I had exhausted all the schools in Tullamore who had me thrown out, one by one, for stealing. It was quite an accomplishment. Patrick was gone so I was completely responsible for my own food supply. She was still beating me as much as ever, perhaps even more now that Patrick was gone. Also I was still being forced into those soiled nappies at night. Therefore I had no option but to keep thieving as much as I could. As a result I was well known to the police for shoplifting as I strove to keep Olive – quite literally – off my back. The Midland Health Board were now involved in my case and after some consideration about my future they decided to send me down to Galway, where I would live in St Joseph's Residential Home for Boys and attend St Patrick's Primary School. Despite my young age I was more than ready to leave my 'home' – of course, I use that term loosely. I don't remember any nervousness at the prospect of heading out into the unknown, all I remember was being very glad to get away from my mother.

Except for those infrequent trips to Dublin to see relatives I had never been out of Tullamore. I knew I was going to miss my brothers and sisters, but that was about it. My first impression of the residential home was a pretty favourable one. As soon as I walked through the front door I could smell food being cooked in the kitchen. To know that I wouldn't have to worry about where and when I was going to get my next meal was a colossal weight off my mind. So I was prepared to enjoy the experience. It was a big building that housed approximately sixty boys of different ages, and was always warm and clean. There were even a few farm animals out the back which we would help out with. We were well looked after, or at least I certainly thought we were, in comparison with what I was used to. There was plenty of food, which I couldn't get enough of. The boys used to laugh at how I would hastily stuff my mouth up at meal times, hardly taking the time to swallow before pushing more food in. I always finished eating first, just in case somebody in charge changed their minds and took my plate away from me.

My social life perked up. I joined the scouts and started to make plenty of friends. Olive had made it almost impossible for Patrick and me to hold on to friends. I was only let out of the house to steal and when I was in the various schools in Tullamore I missed a tremendous amount of days owing to being too bruised to be allowed to join my classmates. For that reason too we never got to know our cousins or relatives in the area. Not only might we have made good friends but, more importantly, we might have been given food. I remember

Patrick being chosen for a small part in the school play. She kept him out of school purposely on the day so that he couldn't take part. This was a complete contrast to how she reacted when any of the others were in a play; she would be excited for them and make sure that they were alright on the night. We figured that she knew there was going to be a big party after the play and didn't want him partaking in the sausage rolls and egg sandwiches. Having the freedom to mix with the other boys was exhilarating. I was grateful for every little thing: for my breakfast, for the warmth of my dormitory, for the fact that someone else washed my clothes and for not being singled out of a crowd for acts of brutality. I learned how to play pool and snooker. All in all my life was pretty normal for the first time ever. There was one Christian Brother who did all the cooking. He was a favourite with the kids and probably influenced my later career choice in catering. I took delight in being asked to help with chopping the vegetables and preparing the soup. It was a new experience to work alongside someone who actually complimented me on what I was doing, instead of Olive standing by, watching me closely, weapon in hand, wanting me to make a mistake so she could beat me. Of course he had no idea about how practised I was regarding household chores and was often surprised at my showing up so regularly to help out.

There was one real downside to this idyll: I had to return to Tullamore every weekend. And I dreaded it. I must have been the only kid in the country who looked forward to Sunday nights and hated Fridays with a passion. From about

Wednesday night onwards I prayed to God that Olive would be a changed woman on my next visit. I never stopped hoping that she might change into a loving mother. If I had only been vaguely aware of how bad my home life was I was now very much aware, thanks to the relative normality of St Joseph's, that it was utterly warped and as far from normal as you could get. After the space of the bigger building I felt almost claustrophobic in the three-bedroomed house now. Plus I was back to being unsure if I was going to get fed on Saturday and Sunday. This basically meant that I had to keep stealing on a regular basis or else the weekends were the usual hell. I either headed into Galway city centre after school and shoplifted little things throughout the week, hiding them away in my locker, or else there was the train journey on the Friday afternoon. Olive told me to keep my eyes peeled for unaccompanied suitcases.

There was a peculiar change in her attitude to me during this time. She began to give me tea and bread at night. I thought that God must have heard my prayers at last and was working overtime to change Olive into a nice mother. Then one evening I drank the last mouthful of tea and discovered five little tablets in the bottom of my cup. When I asked her she told me they were to help me sleep. She refilled the cup with more tea, this time making damn sure that the tablets were fully dissolved, and told me to drink it down. The next time I found the tablets in my tea I fished them out to have a closer look. They had writing down the side, what I took to be their name, 'Roche 5'. I wondered how long she had been drugging me with her 'mad tablets', which is what she called her anti-depressants. In any case she had to stop after I collapsed on the street in Galway and woke up to find myself in hospital. I was kept in for four days, suffering from a pain in my chest and shortness of breath.

Alas St Joseph's and I eventually parted ways. Following a brief stay in Tullamore I ended up in Finglas, in north Dublin, at the St Michael's Assessment Centre for Boys. It was basically a lock-in. The doors were always locked and we never received any visitors. The staff was a mixture of professionals, psychologists, teachers and care workers that concentrated on each individual, assessing his capabilities and personality, in order to be able to develop a plan for his future. I was there for three weeks after which I was given a choice about where I'd like to go next. To help me make my decision I was driven out to see the schools that made it to a shortlist drawn up especially for me. The three alternatives were a school in Clonmel, whose name I have completely forgotten, St Laurence's School in Finglas or Scoil Árd Mhuire in Lusk, County Dublin. I chose the school in Lusk and ended up there for the next two years. The beauty of the surrounding area was what swung it for me. As soon as I saw the green fields I imagined myself running wild and free. It was a tough environment since my fellow students, who came from all over the country, were only there because they had shown themselves to be problematic, or trouble-makers, in one way or another. Nevertheless I was more than happy to be away from my mother and to be fed three times a day.

There were plenty of social outings to keep us occupied. Food was readily available and nobody batted an eyelid if I went back for seconds. When it was fine we were brought fishing. Then, on Friday nights, we were taken into nearby Darndale to attend a local disco. Meanwhile I was busy learning other things from my delinquent colleagues, interesting, and practical things; like how to break into closed stores in the dead of night, and how to rob and drive cars. The latter became a passion of mine. Most of the boys had landed in Lusk after continuous bouts of joyriding sprees, despite getting caught repeatedly, and they were eager to show off their knowledge with hair-raising tales of high-speed chases and races. The last chase of their career, before their arrival in Lusk, was always the best one, with every possible detail concerning the strength of their vehicle, the route spontaneously followed and the inferior driving of the Gardaí – no doubt, miles behind – relayed breathlessly and proudly. They always blamed some little mistake they had made for their eventual capture, never ever allowing for the possibility that they had been out-manoeuvred, or out-driven by the squad cars. It sounded absolutely thrilling and I was a willing student. I learnt how to snap off the wiper from the window of a car, file it down quickly and efficiently, insert it into the ignition, twiddle it around and hey presto! This worked particularly well on Skodas and Mini Minors. Not that I had actually tried putting my knowledge into practice just yet. For now I was happy enough to just listen to the war stories.

Unfortunately I had to visit Tullamore two weekends a month. Actually I was a bit torn about this because I genuinely missed my brothers and sisters. I would have missed Olive too had she let me. After all I was still only thirteen or fourteen years of age. What is interesting is that despite the fact that I was in a school for delinquent boys I was doing my best to go straight. For those weekend visits I would rather use up my precious little pocket money to buy things like soap and washing powder, which I would then pretend to have stolen for my mother. I earned my pocket money by working in the kitchen. It probably wasn't a coincidence that I loved working with food. Years later I read in the school files that *'[Ken] was always trying to buy his parents' affection by bringing home objects he had made.'*

Only when I had no money did I resort to stealing and even then it was the relatively easy feat of walking off the train with someone else's suitcase, preferably a woman's. She was always happy to see the cases, probably because they were like unwrapping an unexpected, and large, present. Rummaging through somebody else's belongings, their clothes, their underwear, perfume and trinkets thrilled her voyeuristic streak. She wasn't above laughing aloud at the owner's taste if it didn't match, or complement, her own. After she had carefully selected what she wanted she told me to burn the case and the unwanted items in the back garden.

# Crime Spree

When I finished my two years at Lusk I returned with a heavy heart to Tullamore. My house parents and teachers had encouraged me to start thinking seriously about a career. They suggested that I try to get into a catering course somewhere as it was something I genuinely liked doing and was good at. Also they pointed out that it was the sort of job you could do anywhere in the world and when I did stop to consider what I might be doing twenty years from now I rather fancied the idea of a life that involved travelling. In the meantime I had to get through the next three months. I spent that summer stealing as much as I could to keep her from beating me. Then I received the news I had been waiting for: I had been accepted to do a cert course in catering at the regional college in County Galway, and I even had my own accommodation laid on for me. I had a room in a house on the Dublin Road, opposite Flannery's Hotel. Unfortunately my newfound wildness caught up with me and within six months of moving to Galway I was joyriding in the way that some people just have to climb mountains or get up on a stage in front of a crowd. It thrilled me, picking a car and taking off down the road without an idea about where I was going; only knowing that I wanted to get there fast. I took to driving as if I had been born to do it. Some joyriders like to wreck their stolen cars, but not me. For me it was all about the mastery of driving as fast as possible without crashing into anything. Most of the time I managed to return the car to the owner's driveway, albeit with an empty petrol tank. That way I wasn't actually robbing cars, merely borrowing them.

One morning I was reefed out of bed at 3 am. The police had come for me. They charged me with robbing seventeen cars. It turned out that my usual accomplice had turned informant on me after he was caught red-handed in a stolen car, telling the police that I had given it to him. I was driven to Dublin in a paddy wagon on the day of my hearing. I think I spent the journey praying I wouldn't be sent back either to Tullamore or to jail. I ended up on remand in St Patrick's Juvenile Delinquent Centre, next door to Mountjoy Jail, where I was utterly miserable for three long weeks. At that time I didn't know anything about my brother Patrick's stay in the same place, but I don't think he hated it as much as I did. The building was cold, damp and smelly while my toilet was a filthy chamber pot with a piece of plywood over it serving as a dodgy lid. By far the worst part for me was the harshness of some of the staff. Maybe some of them hated their jobs. I counted down the hours to my court appearance.

I saw Patsy and Olive as soon as I entered the court room. They were dressed in their best clothes and looked like a very well-to-do couple who were bewildered over their feckless child. I completely ignored them, much preferring to concentrate on the judge.

The judge read out the list of my charges, which included cars I had never touched, but I reckoned it was pointless to get into a debate. Instead I hung my head in genuine shame and told the judge that I was very sorry for my behaviour. He was a kindly man who seemed impressed with my penitence.

'I'm going to give you one more chance, but I promise you, if I ever see you in my court again you will be immediately sent back to St Patrick's. Is that clear?'

I nodded and said 'Yes, Your Honour' at the same time.

It seemed the matter was settled, as far as the judge and I were concerned at any rate. But not everyone was satisfied with the outcome. Just as the judge was about to dismiss me there was a movement from behind and I suddenly heard Patsy's voice.

'Excuse me Your Honour. I'm Kenneth's father and I really feel that he should be locked up for his own good'.

With that his glamorously-dressed wife jumped to her feet, chiming in with her thoughts on the subject, namely that I should be sent to Saint Patrick's until I turned twenty-one. Basically what they had done to Patrick, having him locked up in an asylum so he couldn't breathe a word about the trauma of his childhood. Fortunately the judge turned a deaf ear to them and told me I was free to go. I was brought back to the Garda station to fill out some forms and found my parents sipping tea with the sergeant, who, oblivious to my home life, told me I was a bad lad and had shamed my poor parents. If he only knew the half of it. Olive said something stupid to me, I can't remember what, and I stormed out of the office telling her, Patsy and their new friend that I should have killed myself years ago.

I met my social worker outside who took me to a boys' residential home in Chapelizod. There was no way I was going back to Tullamore. Anyway even if I had wanted to return to the house of horrors my parents wouldn't have stood for it. Instead I was given a bed, clothing and food in the home that was run by a caring, friendly British couple. They provided me with the break I needed, helping me to get a job as a labourer on the building site that was to be the brand new Ilac Centre on Dublin's famous Moore Street. I gave up robbing cars and settled into my new role as a working man with a pay packet. One day I took a walk around the city centre on my lunch break. For the first time I found myself worrying about the future. The home in Chapelizod was more of a half-way house to help troubled boys like myself, so I knew I couldn't stay there forever, but I had no idea how to get myself accommodation, or if I even wanted to stay in Dublin. I found myself standing on O'Connell Bridge and staring idly at two Guinness boats in the distance that were moored across from the Customs House, wondering what it was like to work on a boat. And then it hit me; the most perfect solution to all my problems. If I got a job on a boat I wouldn't have to worry about accommodation. I was delighted with myself.

The next morning I rang the National Union of Seamen and asked for an interview. It was my lucky day. They agreed to interview me, which went very well, and I also passed the medical. So began my new life. I was given a job on the ferry that ran from Rosslare to Pembroke in Wales, straddling two roles as catering assistant and deck hand. The wages were much better than the labourer's pay packet and the hours were much better too. I worked one week on and one week off. It made sense to move with the job so I left Dublin for a room in Rosslare where I lived for the next six months. Then I was put on a new route, the Dublin to Liverpool line. The flexible hours, one week on and one week off, allowed me enough time to indulge in my favourite pastime, drinking heavily. I don't know how I would have made it through my week off had I not been spending most of it drinking myself into a stupor. I wanted to numb myself to my past, to all the violence, to the abuse, to my mother's hatred and this was the perfect way to do it. Soon I was drinking twelve cans of beer a day along with a half litre of Paddy's whiskey.

I collapsed one day and was rushed to Sir Patrick Dunn's hospital, on Lower Grand Canal Street, with bleeding ulcers. (This was the hospital where, maybe sixty years earlier, Countess Markievicz, the most famous revolutionary woman of the Easter 1916 Rising, had died.) Surgery was required, but because I was underage someone had to ring home to get my parents' consent. I gathered the call didn't go too well when a red-faced matron came in to tell me that I had a very sick mother. Apparently Olive refused to believe there was anything wrong with me, refused to give her consent for my operation and then hung up on the speechless woman. I spent the next six weeks in hospital where the doctors managed to cure the ulcers with medication. After umpteen well-intentioned lectures I promised everyone, including myself, that I would give up drinking. Naturally I received no visitors, no 'Get Well' cards and no bottles of Lucozade wrapped up in bright orange paper, but I enjoyed the three meals a day and the peaceful living. On the other hand I fretted about my job and my little room in Rosslare, and with good reason. Six weeks is a long time in the professional world and both were gone by the time I reluctantly left the hospital.

When I rang my boss he apologised, but said he had to give my job to someone else, surely I could understand that he had no alternative. Nevertheless he told me to ring the Seaman's Union. With my experience they would have no problem placing me again. In the meantime, however, I had nowhere to stay. That first night I slept rough behind the hospital. Well, I don't think I actually slept. It was a busy place at night and I was petrified that I'd be seen and sent back to Tullamore. The next day I walked all the way in to St Stephen's Green, figuring that I could spend the night on a bench. All I had was the clothes I was wearing, but I knew I could rob food or anything else I needed. Grafton Street was a very grand and busy street indeed. The shops were all quite upmarket as were the customers who looked a lot more posh than those who shopped on Henry Street. I whiled away the hours watching the ducks in the Green. Quite a few people arrived with loaves of bread and young children in tow. I wished I was a duck: I'd have free bread, all the water I needed and I could fly away to wherever I wanted to. As it began to get dark and the families, young lovers and office workers started to head home I noticed another group of kids, about four or five girls and boys, who looked even more dishevelled than I was. When they saw me staring from my lone bench they came over to ask me who I was.

It turned out they were all homeless, but they boasted to me that they had built their own squat and generously invited me back to stay. It was a little kindness that went a long way. I followed them gratefully to the top of Harcourt Street, to a small rundown building that was right next door to the Eamon Andrews TV Club. Andrews was one of the most popular television presenters on Irish television at this time. This was where they lived. There was a serious downside in that there was no roof and so when it rained, which it did that night, we all got soaked. Nevertheless it was better than the loneliness of a park bench or bush. The ruin became my home for the next few weeks. We worked together as a team, stealing food to survive, pooling our resources. Our life consisted of performing only the barest of essentials. We washed infrequently in public toilets and more frequently got wet at night in the squat. It was a dismal time, although I was glad of the company. I wasn't the only one who had survived a dreadful home life. They all had their own stories of abusive parents, who were too drunk or too angry to care about their kids. Looking back now I appreciate the fact that I never lost hope that things were going to improve for me at some stage. Then I heard about a shelter in Ballyfermot called Sarsfield House. I wasn't satisfied living on the streets, only ever seeing it as a temporary solution, so I applied for a bed and got it. Once I was settled I rang the Seaman's Union again, giving them my new phone number and address. They promised to do their best and get me a job as soon as possible. Three weeks later they rang me with an exciting offer. There was a ship, the *Irish Larch*, docked at Antwerp and they asked me would I like to join her. Would I indeed! The next thing I knew I was boarding a plane to Belgium and life seemed full of potential once more.

I could not believe my luck when I heard where the ship was going. We were sailing to Canada, stopping along the way at ports along the west coast of America. Thanks to Patsy's romantic description of American sunshine, hamburgers and french fries, fast elongated cars and the tallest buildings in the world, I had been longing to see this magical country for years and now here was my chance and I was getting paid for it too. Things were certainly looking up – and they really were until I cocked up royally. We docked at Long Beach, California and while we were there some local market people came onboard to sell their wares. I stole a microphone from one of their stalls. I don't know why I took the stupid thing. I didn't need it, I didn't even want it, but when I thought nobody was watching I reached for it without thinking, possibly just out of habit from a lifetime of stealing, and got caught. If ever there was time that I wished I could turn back time that would be it. The captain had to be told and I was paraded in front of him. I don't think I'll ever forget the look of disgust in his eyes as he told me that once we got back to Ireland I would be paid off the ship. My life as a seafarer was at an end thanks to my own foolish behaviour. I considered my meagre options. Once I walked on to Irish soil I was out of a job, with no place to live. After the luxury of living on a ship the thoughts of returning to a park bench or a roofless building did not appeal to me in the least. Following a lot of inner debate I decided there was only one other place I could go.

Patsy answered the phone and I told him I was ringing from America, and that I was earning fantastic money on the ships and generally having the time of my life. When I suggested that I pay a visit home on my return journey he cheerfully told me to come right ahead. I spent the next couple of hours buying lots of presents for my parents, a necessary tactic. They were actually waiting for me when I got off the ship in Dublin, such was my fancy talk of money and gifts. With my last pay packet in my wallet I was loaded, for the immediate future, and Patsy and Olive seemed genuinely happy to bring me back to their house. They knew nothing about my being fired and I wasn't going to tell them. Back in Tullamore I presented everyone with my peace offerings from America and was free and easy with my money. Sure it was strange being back in that house, but as long as I had money I was treated relatively well. Of course there was always going to be a time limit to my role as generous son who has landed on his feet.

About three weeks later my welcome was officially worn out. I came downstairs one morning to be told by Patsy that he had just got off the phone from the shipping company who had confirmed to him what he had begun to suspect, that my job was no more. There was a distinct chill in the atmosphere. Maybe just two hours after that unpleasant conversation I saw Olive filling a small plastic bag with some of my clothes while Patsy told me to get ready, that we were taking a drive to Dublin. Because I felt I hadn't got another alternative I got into the car and sweated with nervousness for the entire journey. Neither of them spoke until we reached busy O'Connell Street, the heart of Dublin city centre. I didn't know what to expect; jail, school, hospital. Instead Patsy pulled up in front of the General Post Office (GPO) and both of them turned around to me; he to tell me that I was to get out of the car and make my own way from now on; she to bid me a gruff goodbye along with the specific instruction that I was not to contact any of my relatives. This was it. My money had run out and I was being abandoned. There was no point in my pleading or arguing. In fact, I suppose I felt I was getting off rather lightly. Later on, when I found out what happened to Patrick I realised it could have been so much worse. I took my plastic bag and got out of the car. I had no money and absolutely nowhere to go. I stood for a moment, watching my mother and father continue on their way up O'Connell Street, towards Parnell Square, until I could no longer see the car.

'Ah well', I said to myself, 'at least it's not raining.'

I retraced my steps from months earlier and made my way back to St Stephen's Green. There I was very relieved to catch up with some of my homeless friends who encouraged me to try for a place at Hope Hostel on Harcourt Street, which was a shelter specifically for boys. When I walked around to the hostel I found it was run by the house parents that I had in Lusk, a lucky coincidence. They immediately offered me a bed, but explained that I was only allowed to stay there six weeks at a time. Casting around for something a bit more permanent I came up with another wonderful idea a few weeks later. I had befriended an American guy who was also living at the hostel. He was from Boston and like me had been dumped on the streets of Dublin by his own father as soon as they arrived in Ireland. He was desperate to get back to America, but had no money. I felt really sorry for him as he seemed even more lost that I was. At least I was in my own country. He had gone to his embassy in Ballsbridge to explain his story, but even they wouldn't pay his fare home. Meanwhile I had received a lump sum from the tax office and my idea was to pay for my friend to go home to Boston; only I'd get myself a ticket too and go back with him. Perhaps the best part about this plan was that for the first time ever I was able to help someone out in a big way. My friend couldn't believe it when I told him what I was going to do. We began making lots of plans for how we were going to become millionaires in Boston and once again my future was lit up with potential.

I made it as far as Shannon airport. There, two Gardaí boarded the plane looking for me. I should've known it wasn't going to be this easy to escape to a new life. I was told that I never would have been let into America since I was under eighteen years old and only had a one way ticket. This was news to me. With much disappointment over our brutally-dashed plans I wished my friend all the best for the future and got off the plane. He flew on to Boston and I once again considered my options. As far as I was concerned Ireland had nothing for me. I knew I couldn't face returning to Dublin, I never seemed to have much luck in the capital. So I figured I definitely needed a change of scenery and since I couldn't go any farther on my passport, or remaining money, I took a plane to London where I booked myself into a cheap B&B until I could find a cheaper one. After a couple of weeks my money was almost gone and I ended up in the Salvation Army hostel in Whitechapel, London. It was a horrible place for a nervous teenager. Every night there were plenty of sloppy incoherent rows that almost always developed into actual fisticuffs between the many broken-down drunks of all ages, resulting in black eyes or missing teeth. I just kept my head down and hoped no one would take offence to my presence.

One of the staff took pity on me and advised me to go to the dole office and ask about having my rent paid. Next I heard about an Irish hostel on the Holloway Road, and made a rather speedy journey to it, praying I could leave behind the misery of

Whitechapel. I was due some good luck by now and obviously someone else agreed because I managed to get a room at this centre, and then, within days of moving there, I also landed a job with an Irish construction company. It wasn't as nice as working on a ship. I was painting bricks with other Irish lads in the sewers, but it paid very well and I certainly enjoyed the company after work. With a definite pay packet reinstated I was able to over-indulge once more in alcohol. The usual tensions from my not so distant past began to nudge me and I wanted nothing to do with them. They kept dragging me back while I only want to concentrate on moving forwards, on leaving the past in the past. It seemed to me that every time I got myself sorted the memories would start to seep out of the walls, sending me off to stare at them through an empty glass until they were completely distorted, and therefore no longer able to hurt me.

# A New Life

After some months I found that I genuinely missed being onboard a ship so I made what I suppose is a bit of a drastic decision: I applied for and was accepted into the British Merchant Navy. The life of a sailor, with the constant moving around, suited me. It was a life of variety. I got to visit many countries and meet all sorts of people who, for the most part, were escaping something in their past or present. Over the next few years, apart from the necessary heavy drinking, I more or less settled down within myself. By the time I was twenty-two years old I had a nice flat in Hull, Yorkshire, and basically everything I needed. From time to time I wondered how things were in Tullamore, and whether anyone was curious about what had happened to me, until one night I decided to ring my eldest sister. We had a grand chat and I impressed upon her how well I was doing. She told me that Patsy was away in New York, but that she would let him know both that I had called and that I was doing so well for myself. The very next evening a jubilant Patsy rang me from America to tell me that I should come out and join him, that I could definitely earn up to three times the money I was on, up to $1,000 a week, and the living was infinitely cheaper. He made it sound so easy. Furthermore America, the land of high hopes and golden opportunities, was still a huge attraction for me. Plus I have to admit it was kind of wonderful to have my father ringing to ask me to come over and share his life with him. One of my other brothers, Kieran, was already out there with Patsy and I was told that it would be nice for the three of us to spend some time together. So I said 'yes'.

It only took me a couple of weeks to sell off all my possessions and get rid of my little flat. At last I was going to America and not only that, this could be the beginning of a new and healthier relationship with my father. I had always wished he'd take me back with him to the States when I was a child, and now it was actually happening. My expectations were high. I had heard from some pals of mine about befriending their fathers once they had come of age. After the usual clash of the teenage-angst years these boys could now go to the pub with their old man to watch a match, or just chinwag about their jobs and the state of the country. The excitement grew with each day and finally I boarded my plane, confident in the belief that I was leaving my awful childhood and Olive behind forever.

The two of them met me at the airport and brought me back to the apartment that they were renting on the outskirts of New York. I was thrilled at the sight of the yellow taxis, the tall shimmering buildings that gleamed in the sun, the broad streets full of beeping cars, bumper to bumper, and what looked like hundreds and hundreds of people on the paths – or side walks – all seeming to be in the most frantic hurry. When I set down my bags Patsy suggested that I give him all my sterling so he could go to the bank and change it into dollars for me, which made perfect sense. Accordingly I handed over all my savings from selling up my life in the UK, £3,000. A couple of days later I asked him if he had changed my money yet as I literally hadn't a cent to my name. My father shook his head regretfully and explained how he had had to send my £3,000 back to his wife because she had been sick and needed money for her doctor's bills. He promised to make it up to me and handed me $5 to buy myself a pack of cigarettes.

Following a week of having absolutely no money I told Patsy that I was going to head into New York City where I was pretty sure I'd easily pick up a job as a chef. Unwittingly I had forced Patsy to come clean about the reality of my situation. He completely shocked me with the news that I couldn't legally work in America because I didn't have a green card. I had never even heard of this card and was dumbfounded at the idea of having left a well-paid job to come here and now not be able to earn the price of a pint. He assured me that everything would be fine. I could stay and work as long as I got paid under the table, which was my only option since I couldn't apply for a tax number. He told me he had a plan. Accordingly Kieran and I made up flyers, on his instructions, advertising our modestly-priced painting, gardening and electrical services, which we then posted door to door. Well it worked a treat. The work started to flow in and pretty soon my brother and I were working flat out seven days a week. I say my brother and I because we were the ones doing the actual work. Patsy always met with the customer, hammered out the estimate and then appeared a few days later to collect the cheque, only after we had completed the job. While we fulfilled the contracts he went to his maintenance job at a special needs school in the Bronx.

Neither Kieran nor I ever saw a cent of what we were earning and we were the ones pulling in the big money. The wages for the maintenance job were $300, which is what we lived on, as Patsy sent our hard-earned dollars back home to Olive. He kept us in cigarettes and food, but that was all. After a while we were obliged to beg for the money to buy our cigarettes. He even locked the phone into his bedroom so that we couldn't use it. I hated not having my own money after my previous years of independence, but at the same time I had no leisure time to spend any money as we just worked and worked. I guess I just trusted Patsy when he told me that he was going to square things up with me. Time passed quickly. When I had been in America about three months Patsy dropped another bombshell. He was taking himself and Kieran back to Ireland and had already ordered a container to transport his belongings. Not only that, but he was bringing Olive and the two youngest out for a holiday before he left. This was pretty bad news. I had absolutely no inclination to see my mother.

I woke up with an upset stomach on the day of her arrival.

All I could think about was that it had only been seven years since she used to starve and beat me. Patsy went out to collect them at the airport and I didn't bother getting up to greet them when sometime later I heard the key in the door of the apartment. She found me in the sitting room, trying desperately to camouflage my nervousness. Handing me a bottle of my favourite whiskey, Paddy's, she smirked at my surprise, telling me,

'When you were younger you were an awful devil! Sure I could write a book about how bad you were.'

As I write her words down today it strikes me now that it was an odd thing to come out with as an initial greeting. Perhaps it was a poor attempt to apologise for bygones, to joke it off in some way. She hadn't seen me in a few years and now here I was, as far as she was concerned, working hard to keep her in dollars. In fact Kieran and I had probably, unintentionally, paid for her holiday.

I really don't know why Patsy bothered to bring her over. It was a waste of money. She refused to set foot outside the apartment, complaining for days on end that she was too hot to go out and the next day telling us all how she was too afraid of 'coloured people', not that she saw many people sitting in the apartment all day long. I was glad to be kept busy working, staying away from early morning to late at night. A few days later they were all caught up packing for their return to Ireland. Nobody invited me to join them. I really don't think I would have gone with them even if I had been asked, but it would have been nice to have the choice.

About two days before they left Olive cornered me, begging me to ask Patsy to stay on with me in America as she didn't want him back home in the house with her. It was a strange request. There was a time when I would have done anything she asked of me; from stealing packs of tights to lying to a doctor about how exactly I broke my leg. But that time was long gone. The truth was I was very much looking forward to living alone again. I was tired of sharing a small bathroom, tired of having to compromise with the TV remote, and of having to clean up after someone else. Also, and more importantly, with my stingy father out of my hair I could find a cash-in-hand job and this time the cash would actually be going into my hands instead of his. So, for the first time ever, I told her 'no', that I was glad he was leaving as he had just used Kieran and me and as a result of working seven days a week for him I was penniless.

As it was he left me with nothing. He had rented an empty apartment, which was cheaper than a furnished one and he pretty much left the apartment as he found it. The container he ordered was massive, eighteen feet long. I hadn't even a pillow to rest my head against by the time they left to go to the airport. He brought everything back home, including all the furniture bought with the money that Kieran and I earned, not bothering to ask me how I was fixed or if I wanted to hold on to my cheap pillow. I remained in New York for a few months after they left, continuing on with the work single-handedly, renovating houses and building decks. It was tough without Kieran and I realised that I couldn't continue indefinitely like this. For one thing I was struggling with my back. It was also seasonal work; I certainly didn't fancy trying to work outdoors in a New York winter. Besides I would much prefer to be working in a kitchen.

After asking around I decided to head to Boston and try my luck there. There was a bigger Irish population in Boston, or so I was told, and therefore it would be easier to pick up a better kind of cash-paying job. My plan regarding job hunting in Boston was pretty straightforward: I simply entered the first decent Irish pub that I came across. Sure enough I got chatting to the owner, telling him about my marvellous cooking abilities and promising him that I would bring in Irish customers. He was persuaded to give me a shot, shaking my hand in agreement over the rate per hour, handing over the running of his food section to me. It was a busy pub and I basically worked and drank hard in equal measures. I also got sorted regarding accommodation, taking a room in a house with people who hailed from Tullamore, of all places. Although I considered myself a bit of a loner I did enjoy the social aspect of my new job and was always interested in hearing how things were back in Ireland from the constant stream of Irish tourists. A couple of months later I got talking to a regular customer, a guy from Kilbeggan, in County Westmeath. It turned out he knew Patsy, having worked with him some years ago in Ireland. He asked where Patsy was now and did I think he'd be interested in coming to Boston. The guy was a foreman for a south Boston company and they were in dire need of an experienced electrician. I hadn't spoken to my parents in over two years, but I promised Patsy's old colleague that I'd give him a ring to see if he'd be interested. Looking back now I'm not sure why I rang home. Maybe I just like to get on with people and accommodate them as best I can, which is basically what I was doing for my customer. He needed an electrician? Well I could try and help him out there. On the other hand, perhaps I was waiting for a good excuse to contact the house in Tullamore and let them know that I was still in America after all this time; that things had worked out well for me. It's a strong possibility that I was still looking for validation from my parents about the life I was leading, in spite of everything. I think deep down we all want our parents to be proud of us. If we're not looking for their approval then we are probably hoping for their respect – at the very least.

Patsy was very excited about the job. He remembered the guy and told me to tell him that he would be in Boston as soon as he could get the airfare together. Then he rang me back the following day, obviously having thought about the matter, and discussed it with his wife, to ask me outright would I send him the plane ticket, plus a second one for Kieran. Instead of saying 'no', or saying I hadn't got that kind of money, which I hadn't, I told him that I'd see what I could do. Big mistake, but as always I was easily charmed, or manipulated, by my father. He just knew how to sweet talk me. I forgot about the New York fiasco, the lack of wages and my nabbed pillow. As it happened I suppose I was feeling a bit homesick. In fact, to be honest, I found myself missing my family. Since arriving in Boston I had wasted hours and hours of my life, when I couldn't sleep or else was maudlin after a lot of whiskey, wishing that my past was a vastly different one from the reality because I would have much preferred to be living and working in Tullamore, surrounded by everyone I knew.

The life of an illegal immigrant is a strange one. You can't take a holiday, can't allow yourself to get sick or else you'll lose out in your pay packet. The fact that you really shouldn't be where you are prevents you from feeling settled or feeling like you truly belong, no matter how much you love your informally-adopted country. You can't vote or open a bank account and you live with the niggling worry of getting caught and being flung out of your new home forevermore.

My father's sweet talk consisted of telling me that it would be great to be all together again. I rang him from the bar during my break and the line was so good it was like he was standing in front of me. He added that it was more than time that we started working on repairing our broken-up family, that it would be nice if we all got along and developed a real closeness. I nodded my head in agreement. It was exactly what I wanted to hear.

I was now in a bit of a dilemma. My one-roomed bedsit was far too small for three people so I decided that I'd better get a bigger place. Only I couldn't afford a deposit for a bigger apartment on my modest wages so I borrowed money from several different friends until I had a grand total of $5000. I exchanged my cosy bedsit for the more expensive two-bedroomed apartment, used $500 of the loan to buy my father a second-hand car and – last but not least – I dutifully sent off the two plane tickets to Tullamore as requested. I must admit that I felt very proud of myself for setting everything up.

I arranged to pick them up from Logan Airport in Boston, on their arrival date, along with Patsy's mate who offered to come out with me. He was going to give my brother a job too and was anxious to meet him. We got there on time and positioned ourselves in Arrivals where we must have seen every single person who was on their Aer Lingus plane. As the minutes ticked by I began to think they must have lost their luggage until we spotted the air hostesses and the pilot. Something was wrong. I approached one of the air hostesses and asked her was there anyone left on the plane, but of course there wasn't. Next I went up to the Aer Lingus desk, gave them the names of my father and brother, and asked them could they give me any information on their whereabouts. I watched the girl tap in the letters of their names and then hit a few more buttons on her keyboard. I had already explained that they were my flesh and blood so it's no wonder she looked surprised when she discovered that my dear old Dad had handed in his Boston plane tickets at New York and bought himself two tickets to Phoenix, Arizona, instead. I couldn't believe my ears and asked her was she sure, asked her could she check her information again. But she was 100 per cent sure. There was a screeching sensation in my brain as I struggled to keep calm in front of the guy from Kilbeggan. I fought the urge to sit down on the ground and cover my face with my shaking hands. Once again I had allowed my father to fool me. He had just used me to get the free tickets. More than anything else; the anger, the embarrassment; I couldn't get over how hurt I felt. Surely he couldn't hurt me any more than he already had.

Patsy's mate looked mystified, as if the world, and me, had suddenly gone crazy. He was standing right beside me trying to digest the fact that he had been inexplicably stood up. But at least he wasn't family. At least he didn't owe $5000. At least it wasn't personal. What could I say to him by way of explanation? It was a long, uncomfortable walk back to the car. I awkwardly asked to be dropped off at the pub where I worked. He jerked his head quickly, in acquiescence, without looking at me. We hardly spoke on the drive back. I had plenty of time to try and remember exactly how many people I had told about my father and brother coming over from Ireland to stay with me, how many people I was now in debt to, how much time and money went into stocking up my big refrigerator. A few short hours later I was bitterly drunk, alternating between tears of rage and tears of sorrow.

When I got back to my new – and now definitely unaffordable – apartment I rang the house at home, but nobody answered – for the next three hours. Olive was there and purposely not picking up in case it was me, I just knew it. Determined to confront at least one of my parents, and get to the bottom of this, I rang the police station in Tullamore, pretending that my mother was sick and I was worried because the phone was off the hook. A very helpful Garda told me that he'd go around to the house immediately, and to give him ten minutes before dialling the number again. I swallowed a beer whole while I waited. This time, when I rang, she picked up. I dispensed with the small talk,

'Where are they?'

'Oh it's you. Your father said he'd give you a ring later. He met someone on the plane who offered him big money for a job in Phoenix.'

'Why didn't he ring me immediately and let me know?'

'I just told you. He said he's ringing you later.'

He never called me. Over the next couple of days I sank into a bad depression and went on a bit of a binge. The heightened humiliation and foggy solutions that come from drinking with a vengeance prompted me to leave Boston behind – the job, the big apartment and my generous friends whom I just couldn't face. I ran away to Florida where I drank heavily, sampling all the local bars.

When I eventually returned to Boston I set up a home renovations business. Over the next few years, I managed to pay off every last cent of that $5,000.

# Betrayed by the System

In 2002 the pain in my back was getting increasingly worse. I had an idea about what caused it and when I told my doctors here in New Jersey about the beatings and starvation they encouraged me to get my medical files from Ireland. Apart from the obvious damage resulting from hours of my childhood spent strapped across a table while being battered by a cheese board, there was also the fact that Olive sometimes took a fancy to making Patrick and I walk on our toes for hours around the house. Now I had absolutely no idea what information was available, having never seen a medical file before, and was in no way prepared for what I read. Thanks to the Freedom of Information Act 1997 hundreds of pages were sent to me across the ocean detailing the abusive childhood that Patrick and I were subjected to as very young children. It was an incredible discovery and a chilling one as it became obvious to me that people knew or suspected what was going on and I felt that no one, including the Midland Health Board, did anything significant to make our lives better.

There it was, our childhood in print, in letters, memos, case histories and reports: Patrick's scavenging from bins, all my visits to hospitals including those for malnutrition, the fact that our mother was 'fixated' on us, and that our father knew she wasn't feeding us. I read about my being hospitalised just after Christmas, on the last day of 1969. The registrar at Tullamore Hospital filled out my form, writing that I had been brought in suffering from malnutrition and inflammation of the toes – thanks to those freezing mornings spent scrubbing everybody's shoes in our back garden – which was believed to be a result of 'ill-treatment at home'. One of the biggest surprises was that Patsy knew so much. For years Patrick and I had believed she had fooled him while he was away in America. In fact he had repeatedly looked for help, including going to the local priests to ask them to talk to his wife. A social worker provided a detailed study of my misery as far back as 1976, the starvation and the violent treatment. Why were we not taken from Olive? At some point it was suggested that we should be removed to a foster family, but nothing came of it. This went some way to explaining why Patsy's behaviour became more aggressive to us over the years. Perhaps when he saw the lack of reaction from the authorities to his revelations about Olive's treatment of us, he decided that maybe she had a point.

Social workers visited our house once a week for years. Just recently, in 2009, a mother was jailed for her neglect and abuse of her six children. Social workers visited that house in County Roscommon twice a week, according to media reports. The days that the social workers called were the only days that those kids got to eat biscuits.

Possibly as a result of my hospital stays my mother was obliged to take me to the Midland Health Board where I would be weighed and measured. Naturally on our way to the centre she would warn me not to tell them anything, adding that anything I said would be repeated back to her and that she would kill me when we got back to the house. She needn't have bothered with her threats since I did not get a fighting chance to rat her out. Although they went to the bother of weighing me I was never directly asked about my eating habits at home. To be sure Olive had covered all the bases. She told the staff that I would get sick if I ate any sweets, making sure that I couldn't be bribed to give out any information against her. She also told the social workers that I was refusing to eat. And nobody thought to ask me otherwise.

Friday was a common day for visits and that became our 'safe' day, when we were dressed up and paraded as normal members along with the rest of the family. If it happened that we were black and blue from a beating – and it happened many times – she would merely lock us up in our bedroom, tie us to the furniture and gag us, to be sure to be sure. And it was as simple as that. The social workers, who included nuns, would politely enquire into our whereabouts only to be bluntly told that we had been sent off for a day of fishing complete with packed lunches provided by that stalwart of motherhood, Olive. We could hear the conversation from our 'cell'. Like all important visitors they were brought into the orange-carpeted front room of stolen treasures to take their tea, beneath the picture of President John F. Kennedy, and make tentative small talk with a fearless Olive. They looked as scared of her as we were.

Once I got over my initial shock at what the documents contained, I wanted to do something about it. I rang the police station in Tullamore and told them I wanted to make a statement in relation to my mother, Mrs Olive Doyle. I didn't receive a very positive reaction and so I sent on copies of the files to give them a taste of the evidence in my possession. A detective asked me why I was only coming forward now and I told him that no one would have believed me until now. It took me more than two years to gain the release of my files from the Midland Health Board. I can only feel that they were trying to hide how much they knew about me and my brother, and how little they did. Patrick and I have hundreds of pages of documentation in our hands today, but we know there are more out there.

I rang Patrick's house on 24 August 2002. It was about 4 am in Swansea, but I couldn't wait any longer. We hadn't spoken to one another in years. Our parents had made sure of that, and now we couldn't stop. Although our lives had turned out very differently, in that Patrick was happily married with children and grandchildren, and I had never even held a girl's hand, we were overawed by the dismal similarities. We had both been personally ushered out of that house in Tullamore by Olive and Patsy, into institutions. Patrick was made to sign himself in to a mental institution despite the fact that a doctor was on record as saying that he was not mentally unstable. He was there for months before a psychiatrist wrote pushing for his release. Meanwhile I ended up in crazy situations, attending a wide variety of schools, after being expelled for stealing food. Again I ask the obvious question, how come none of the teachers and the many school principals could probe further into why on earth I was stealing so much food?

Over the years we had seemingly gone back to Patsy and Olive for more of the same. Neither of us was capable of cutting ourselves off permanently from our parents, each hoping desperately for some sort of breakthrough, to be allowed to form a normal relationship with them, which never happened. We had both been homeless, and had both been addicted to alcohol, which we used to stem the horrific memories and the sensations they produced, a habit we had now both kicked. We both suffered from severe depression, severe pain in our spines and both saw our mother in our dreams – when we were able to sleep, that is; an irregular accomplishment because we were both suffering from Post-Traumatic Stress Disorder. In a pathetic way it was a mutually beneficial conversation. Being able to pool the information on our illnesses, on how Olive's brand of mothering continued to plague us from day to day, despite the fact that we were grown men, showed me that I wasn't simply a nutcase who cried like a baby when I had nightmares and continued to wet the bed on the really bad nights. There was comfort to be taken in that my behaviour was not unique to me, and that my brother Patrick, who had shared my childhood experiences, was going through the exact same thing. We took strength from one another and discussed what we would do next.

I told Patrick that I wanted to go public with our story; that I could not permit Olive to take her dreadful secrets to her grave. She had made us suffer so much as kids, and we were still suffering as men. Now, it was her turn. But first I was going to give our mother a fighting chance to defend herself by explaining to me why she had done what she had. I wanted to confront her and Patsy with what I knew. Patrick wished me luck and said he'd be waiting to hear what they said. We were both especially curious about Patsy's reaction. The files showing him looking for help for us had thrown us and neither of us were too sure how we now felt about him. On the one hand he had tried to do something, tried to involve the authorities in our distress, while on the other hand he still went off to America every year knowing we had nobody to protect us.

Olive answered the phone when I rang. A lot was riding on this call. If she had been straight with me then I probably wouldn't have pursued the route I have. However it wasn't a very enlightened conversation, in fact it was the exact opposite of what an enlightened conversation should be. She was her usual flippant self, totally uninterested or certainly pretending to be completely unmoved by my theme. I told her about the documents, and the information that had come to light, adding that I needed to ask her a few questions.

'Fire away.'

I asked her pointedly why she had hated me so much, why

she had deprived me of food. She made her immediate reply in a merry vein,

'Oh Ken, you did not like food.'

I asked her why she beat me almost every day of my life.

'You were bold.'

I asked her why she broke my leg.

'It was self-defence.'

Giving up on her I asked to speak to Patsy. As it happened he was already listening in on the extension. He refused to discuss any abuse, telling me that he was retired now and that it was all 'water under the bridge'. In other words he was letting Patrick and me down once more. Before he hung up on me he told me never to ring the house again. A few hours later he rang Patrick. Obviously our parents saw him as an easy target, the soft one who would cave in to their demands. Patsy was beside himself with rage, shouting down the phone at the top of his voice,

'You fucking bastard! I hope you're happy now. Your mother has just had a massive heart attack and may not see the day through.'

Patrick was understandably shocked, but managed to tell Patsy that he really didn't know the half of it, just how much she had tortured us while he was away in another country. His father, however, was adamant that he did not want to hear a word of it.

'Under no circumstances am I going to listen to any of these allegations that you are making. I am standing by your mother one hundred per cent. You better go get yourself some evidence.'

When I rang the hospital in Tullamore there was no record of a Mrs Doyle being rushed in with a cardiac arrest. I told Patrick not to worry, assuring him that she wasn't dying and that we had plenty of evidence between us. We spoke a lot over the next few weeks as we both absorbed our files and digested just how many people could have done something to help us, but didn't. It was a very sobering experience and one that led us both to wonder how many kids are out there still suffering because of the inadequacies of the Irish social care system. In 2003, not too long after receiving all the files on my own childhood abuse, I turned on my television in New Jersey and watched the latest breaking news story. Four children had been rescued from a house, which was approximately three miles from where I lived, by child protection services. Just like Patrick and I the kids had been visited by social workers once a week over a period of time before something was eventually done. They had been adopted by a woman who was only interested in the money she got for taking them in. The eldest was an eighteen-year-old boy who weighed approximately 70 lbs. It turned out that the authorities were spurred into action after the four children were found eating out of bins. When questioned by police, the woman explained that the reason they were so underweight was because they all suffered from an eating disorder. Does this sound familiar? The 'mother' got six years behind bars while the four children were paid $11 million by the State of New Jersey as compensation for the mistakes they had made.

I rang the *Sunday World* newspaper an hour after I spoke to my parents and asked them if they would be interested in hearing our story. I chose this paper because I knew it was a favourite in the Doyle household. If Patsy and Olive had been more co-operative, if even one of them had acknowledged what Patrick and I had been through, I don't think I would have made this call. But they hadn't wanted to talk and I was determined to blast the doors and windows of that hell house open for good. From now on there would be no more secrets. Patrick and I could no longer be her reluctant accomplices in helping her stand guard over the evil truth. It was no surprise when Patrick confided in me that he had never even told his wife, Berny, the real extent of the brutality. It was time to get organised. I got myself a plane ticket to Dublin airport where I was going to finally meet up with my big brother after twenty-two years, my plane arriving in ten minutes after his. We were also going to be met by a journalist from the *Sunday World*, plus a photographer, both of whom would be accompanying us to Tullamore, where detectives were waiting to interview us separately about our mother. The prospect of what we were about to do was both terrifying and exhilarating. Olive's day of reckoning was at hand.

# Reunited

I saw him through the crowds first and shouted out 'Doyle!' It was 2002, we had both aged and put on a lot of weight, which made us laugh shyly. Patrick was carrying a smart-looking case and I kidded him about it, just like when we were kids and had stolen something flashy.

'I like your briefcase. Where did you nick it from?'

It broke the ice and we hugged briefly, grinning at one another as we never had when we were sharing a bedroom/torture chamber. James McDonald and Val Sheehan, the journalist and photographer, who were waiting for us in Arrivals, greeted us warmly. They took us back to their office to let us change out of our travelling clothes and get something to eat before the 120 mile drive to Tullamore. I must admit my stomach was churning for the last few miles of that drive, but James kept us busy talking, asking us plenty of questions about the area. It was late by the time we reached the Garda station, just after 9 pm. The old police station that we knew so well was gone and in its place was a bigger, modern building. When we went in we were given a meal after our journey. Then Patrick and I were led off in different directions, our interviews only beginning around 10 pm. I remember thinking that this would be the first time that I was going to tell the truth in a police station, having lied so many times to cover for Olive when I had been caught thieving. It was a marathon interview session, with the detectives involved having to pull a double shift for a whopping eight hours of questions, finally stopping at 6 am the following morning. Everyone was exhausted. It had been a difficult night at times, remembering stuff that I had done my best to forget, reliving my fears in front of the detectives who were plainly shocked at some of the events. The sun was up and the birds were singing when we were both congratulated by the guards for telling the truth, for presenting two separate stories that completely corroborated one another.

The story hit the paper a few weeks later on 1 September 2002. I was back home in America, where I bought a copy at the airport, thousands of miles away from the epicentre of grief. For that reason it hit Patrick harder than it did me. Plus he had to cope with the reactions of his wife, his kids and his wife's shocked family who had had no clue as to why he caused their daughter so much trouble with his sudden addictions to drink and then drugs. Seeing the large, close-up photo of Olive on the paper's front page was an eerie experience. Neither of us felt triumphant, it was just something we had to do. After the story broke a former school teacher contacted the police to say that he had heard the stories, at the time, of us being starved and subjected to cold baths. A former school nurse revealed that she remembered the bruises on my body.

Once again Patsy took a last pot shot at Patrick, ringing him on the morning the paper came out to tell him that his mother lay dying in Tullamore Hospital after a massive heart attack. Once again, when I rang the hospital, there was no record of a dying Mrs Doyle. He ended his call by telling him that he and I were no longer part of his family.

Oh, Daddy dearest, we never were part of the family.

✉ ✉ ✉

Two years after the story broke in the *Sunday World*, our brother Michael killed himself. It was Michael who risked God knows what by sneaking food to Patrick and me when we were kids. He used to receive a terrible taunting from our mother who nicknamed him 'Pissy' because he frequently wet the bed and 'Four Eyes' because he wore glasses.

# Part Four:

# Patrick

OFFALY COUNTY COUNCIL 40

PUBLIC HEALTH DEPARTMENT
COURTHOUSE
TULLAMORE

REF.........

9th January, 1970.

Hospitaller Order of St. John of God,
Child Guidance Clinic,
Orwell Road,
Rathgar,
Dublin.

Re:- Patrick Doyle, 3, Pearse Park,
Tullamore, your ref: 753/10/222.

Dear Brother

The abovementioned attended the Child Guidance Clinic on 21/11/1969 and to date I have not received a report. Will you kindly let me have a report.

Psychiatric Social Worker at the Clinic rang to-day and she informed me that she wishes Patrick to attend again and also his brother Kenneth. Apparently the father mentioned about Kenneth when he attended with Patrick on 21st November.

I have requested the father to let me know if he will agree to bring Patrick and Kenneth to the clinic if appointments are made and I will write to you again if he agrees.

# Living with Post-Traumatic Stress Disorder

I take twenty-seven tablets every single day to combat the mental and physical effects of our childhood. My illnesses include severe and frequent depression, severe and frequent anxiety and a spinal injury (*ostrio parosis*) for which I undergo therapy on a weekly basis.

In 1990 I had a fit. To be honest I'm not sure what happened exactly or what was going through my mind, and I still can't explain it. It was the month of June, a gorgeous summer's day, when I took a hatchet to the bedroom that I shared with my wife. She was forced to call the police because I was out of control and she was afraid that I was going to hurt myself. When they arrived I was politely asked to vacate the house so that Berny could get herself and the kids out safely to her parents' place. The house was still when I returned. Everyone had dropped what they were doing when I went mad. There were dishes on the table, toys everywhere and the washing machine needed to be emptied, its cycle finished just moments before I walked back through my front door. I ignored the mess and headed upstairs to the room I had attacked.

I emptied it of furniture, ornaments, pictures, carpet, leaving only the double mattress on the bare floor. I emptied it too of sunlight, nailing two continental quilts across the window so that there wasn't the slightest hint of the summer outside. While my neighbours mowed and watered their thirsty lawns, washed their cars or sat on dusty deck chairs, drinking cups of tea and fanning themselves with their newspapers, I hammered the bedroom door into its frame, making an eight inch hole in the bottom of the door so that food and drink could be passed through to me. During the day I blocked up the hole with cardboard.

The family returned to the house and typically gave me the space I craved. The kids, coached by their resilient mother, resigned themselves to talking to me through the hatch. For weeks on end I did nothing more than lie on the bed and grow a beard. I was out of my mind with fear, too scared to leave the bedroom, and what was much worse was the fact that I was completely without any understanding for what I was going through. The only light I could cope with was a candle in a jam jar. I do remember praying, asking God to take me. When that didn't get me anywhere I decided to do it myself.

Everyone had gone out to the park and I stood in the bare cell, which had once been my cosy bedroom, clutching the cord of Berny's nightgown, shaking and bitterly unsure of myself. I threw it over the notch above the window, made a noose with my trembling hands and placed it around my neck. Now all I needed to do was confirm to myself that I was absolutely doing the right thing. I wanted to be sure. And that was the hard part; I couldn't decide one way or another. It was very confusing. I couldn't even make up my mind whether I wanted to laugh or cry. A voice in my head yelled at me to do it while I heard myself timidly say, 'I can't'. The cord was tight around my neck and I still couldn't make the final decision, much too frightened now to kill myself and, at the same time, appalled by my lack of courage. A film played out on the wall in front of me. I watched my wife and kids return to find my lifeless body hanging from the window. I saw Berny in hysterics, screaming at my bewildered sons and daughters,

'We shouldn't have left him; I told you we shouldn't have left him.'

I pushed my homemade noose over my head, pulled back the quilt, opened the window and threw the cord into the garden next door. For the next few hours I cried and cried, pacing the room wrapped in a sheet, completely disorientated and devastated by sheer exhaustion. Whatever it was, the madness that had overtaken me, I could feel it trickle out with my tears until I was able to call my son Patrick, telling him to bring me the hammer so that I could release myself from my prison. They all gathered around me as I stepped over the threshold that had kept them from me. My reflection in the mirror was almost unrecognisable to me, I had lost lots of weight and my beard was practically sitting on my chest. Berny tried to hold back her tears while our youngest, Sean, handed his smelly and dishevelled father a bar of chocolate he had bought for him a few days earlier.

I would love to be able to tell you that that was that. But I can't. For days afterwards I was too scared to go to the bathroom by myself, convinced that four men were lying in wait for me. My wife had to accompany me. To this day I have to leave the bathroom door halfway open, whether I'm using the toilet or having a shower. My family are well used to this now and know to call up the stairs,

'Is it alright to come up?'

To this day when I get up from my chair to go the bathroom Berny automatically jumps up and comes with me, talking to me throughout from the next room, keeping me occupied. A lot of bad things have happened to me in bathrooms, in Tullamore and in institutions.

I see my brother a lot, maybe thirty or forty times a week. He's a grown man now, in his forties, and lives in America, but that doesn't matter. I constantly see him around my house. In my mind's eye he's a terrified child again, completely malnourished and desperately afraid. I see his naked and bruised body lying shivering in my bath. When I go to bed at night I have to leave a light on because I don't want to step on little Ken who I see lying naked on the floor and tied to my bed. If I go to a supermarket and stop anywhere near the rows of uncooked chickens waiting to be bought and consumed, I suddenly see Ken in front of me, huddled over as he eats, sucking the marrow out of the chicken bones that I've brought back for him. He is so skinny and weak that I'm constantly afraid he's going to die, that I'm not trying hard enough to get him food.

Because of all these memories, or flashbacks, I find it easier sometimes to stay in bed where I won't see the bath or chickens or over-flowing bins filled with stale and dangerously smelly foodstuffs. Accordingly I will, from time to time, spend three to four days a week under the covers, doing my very best to keep the memories at bay using sleep. During these bouts of depression I can't bear daylight or people, including those I love, around me. So the continental quilt goes back over the window and I refuse all company except when it's Berny bringing me my cornflakes, cup of tea and medication. It's hard on her. She begs me to get up and join her downstairs, but I just can't.

I can't even begin to calculate what my childhood has cost her, or describe what I owe her. There are simply no words.

Sometimes I will get up at 2 or 3 am and put on five, maybe six, loads of washing. Then I will carry the wet clothes out to the garden and hang them on the line as quietly as I can. After all it's not even 5 am and I don't want to disturb my neighbours. Our bathroom must be the cleanest in the street thanks to my need to scrub it every day. I won't let any of my kids clean it because I don't want them doing anything I was made do when I was a child. I just can't seem to break these patterns from when Olive forced me do the housework. Another pattern is my embarrassment over being 'caught' by Berny when I take food. I will go to the cabinet and if Berny suddenly walks in I feel like I'm doing something bad. More often than not I will ashamedly put the food back, asking her

'Am I being greedy?'

She does her best to convince me otherwise, but I still often feel that I'm being a greedy pig, eating food just because I want to. Olive never allowed me near her presses except when she wanted to taunt me with food by having me clean them out for her. If I dared to ask her for a slice of bread or a drink of water she would beat me. I know it upsets Berny when I ask her can I take something to eat, but once again I can't seem to stop myself from doing it.

I have to check our bins every day to make sure that no food has been thrown out. Again this is just something that I have to do. If I find anything I'll put it out for the birds because I can't bear to see them scrape around the garden for food. The thought that there are lots of scared children out there going through what I went through makes me want to scream with rage. If I'm out on the street, or in a shopping centre, and I see a mother smack her child I have to keep a hold of myself or else I'm afraid I'll march over and start shouting abuse at the woman. I cannot stand to see children being hit even if it's just a light slap. I constantly daydream about saving all the abused kids in the world. To this end, I suppose, I became a member, about fourteen years ago, of the Swansea branch of the National Society of Prevention of Cruelty to Children. Reading their monthly newsletter, from cover to cover, usually sends me into a depression that can last several days.

I would never have believed that my childhood could affect my adulthood so much. It seems to get worse the older I get. I dread opening my eyes in the morning because I dread the daily assault of memories and visions. At 7.30 am I'll take my medication, unless I manage to stay in bed and sleep until the afternoon, which I like to do as it makes the day go in faster. The idea of giving up occurs to me about twenty, twenty-five times a week. I don't want this fear to be my life; I don't want this to dominate my old age. I guess the fearful feeling is what I was avoiding when I drank and then took drugs. But I am determined to keep going. I've come too far now to give up. My wife has been brave for me; my kids have been brave for me, so I must be brave for me.

Mother's Day is another problem day for me – countless adverts on the TV that suggest that we all have loving mothers when I know better. I see her everywhere too. The visions are as real as this pen I am using to write these words, as real as my fear about what I'm looking at. My body shakes all over and I feel my heart racing even though I know it's all in my head. Sometimes I see the two of them. I'll see her walk across my living room with a terrified Ken tied to her wrist, just the way she used to keep us tied to her body after she had beaten us black and blue. Two days ago I watched her arrange a vase of flowers on the dining table. She never leaves me alone. I see her drop things on the floor – letters, clothes, my tablets. When I can't see her I hear her calling my name. It is time for a beating. I wake up sweating in the middle of the night to see her running silently around my bed, her eyes fixed on mine as she flashes me a ferocious smile before turning and disappearing out the door. She is always dressed the same, her blue housecoat and black leggings. Over her arm is the old yellow tea-towel that she used to carry with her about the house.

My body is like a photo album, only instead of images I have marks to remind me of certain days that I'd rather forget. I have a five inch scar on my left leg. Olive sent me to the shops one afternoon, telling me to bring back a quarter pound of sliced ham. The simple task was made very difficult by the fact that I hadn't eaten in a few days and the smell of the meat almost made me swoon. With both my eyes and mouth watering I couldn't resist taking a piece; surely, I thought, she'd hardly miss one thin slice. I was wrong. She ripped the top of my left leg with a long piece of wood that had a nail stuck in it. By the time she was finished there was blood everywhere. The cut was so deep I could actually see the muscle. I was only twelve, but I knew that I needed to go to the hospital to have it stitched. Instead she got me to wrap a sock around my leg, using duct tape to hold it against my skin. It took weeks for the wound to heal. I was instructed to tell anyone who asked that I slipped and fell on glass while playing in the back garden.

It's not just Olive who haunts me. I still hear, from time to time, the distressed cries of my fellow patients in the psychiatric hospital. I'm sure things there are a lot better now but I only have the blackest memories. In some ways those patients, who seemed to me to be too drugged up to defend themselves, remind me of vulnerable children today. Like Ken and I they couldn't go outside to play. Like Ken and I they spent a lot of their time locked up. Like Ken and I nobody seemed to care about them. It was a place of fear, especially for those who understood enough to be afraid. Of course waking up to the distinct possibility of violence was just like a typical day in the Doyle household. At least I could expect to eat regularly in hospital, even if I was completely denied my freedom.

Maybe I know why I sometimes can't bear to see the sunlight. Today when the sun streams through my window I remember exactly what it felt like to be tied to the handle of the bedroom window on a summer's day. Because of the glorious weather Olive would leave Ken and me behind as she took the rest of her brood out for a picnic in the park. If someone chanced to ask her where we were she would tell them that we had gone to visit our father in America. That someone, a neighbour or a friend of ours, would be understandably envious of our holiday and utterly oblivious to our true surroundings. If only they could have seen us. Two boys, aged somewhere between four and eleven years, covered in bruises, tears, starkly underweight, naked, and bound by a pair of Dunnes Stores' extra large Sun Haze nylons to their bedroom window. The house is deathly silent so they can plainly hear the kids playing outside in the sunshine, in the back lane behind the house, shrieking as they chase one another or else knocking about with a football for hours. Perhaps it is June and the older kids are out with their new tennis racquets, hyped up from watching the stars at Wimbledon. Or maybe it's a bunch of very young girls clattering around in their mother's shoes, pushing dolls in their squeaky prams, as they scold imaginary children. From where they are crouched the boys can see a patch of the brightest blue, but they are too tired to even wish they could be out beneath that sky running around with their friends. It has been a few days since they last ate and their energy levels are low, so much so that, despite the fact it's a warm, sunny day, they feel a dreadful chill.

# Afterword

I remember my father's father visiting our house, loaded down with vegetables from his garden. Olive told him to fuck off, that she didn't want or need his food. She knew it was just a ruse to check up on her and us. As it happened he arrived just minutes after Ken and I had received another hiding. Noticing our tears and umpteen bruises in a variety of colours – green, yellow and blue – he turned to her and told her something neither of us has ever forgotten,

'Be careful, Mrs Doyle. Those two boys will return one day and you'll be sorry.'

# Appendix

This appendix contains medical records, letters from social workers and health boards, psychologists' reports and case studies on Ken and Patrick Doyle.

Names of personnel have been removed.

1969 TWO OF THREE

# NOTES

REGISTER NO. ........................ FRIEND'S ADDRESS ........................ (2)

31. XII. 69.
Vomited once tonight
Father says that child is neglected – only getting one meal / day.

O/E T° 101.5°F P. 120/min
Child emaciated – not dehydrated
Quite an intelligent little boy.

Abdomen: H/S ✓ Tongue moist
pot-belly
Bt. bowels okay
No wasting
Chest clear No cough or chest colds
DIET.......... no glands Δ Malnutrition – neglect.
Sepsis toe both feet.

| DATE | TREATMENT (Including Extra Diet and Stimulants) | DATE | TREATMENT (Including Extra Diet and Stimulants) |
|---|---|---|---|
| | Rx Food ++ | | |
| | Vitamins | | |
| | Calogen | | |
| | 1. Weigh → 27¼ lb | | |
| | 2. X-RAY: Chest | | |
| 5/1/70 | 2nd, 3rd toes on lt. side are infected – blistering. | | |
| | H/D ... cicatrin powder | | |
| [illegible]/1/70 | May go home | | |
| | To attend [illegible] clinic. | | |
| NB | next clinic | | |

FILM DATE please

(B)

AGE 6 YEARS OLD 27¼ LBS

ABOVE
FATHER SAYS CHILD IS NEGLECTED and is ONLY GETTING ONE MEAL PER DAY HOSPITAL ADDMITTANCE FOR MALNUTRITION. (5)

Patient notes on Ken Doyle, 31 December 1969

9th February, 70.

Tullamore.

Re: Kenneth Doyle, 3, Pearse Park, Tullamore.

Dear Dr.

This patient was admitted on the 31st December suffering from malnutrition and inflammation of the toes which were believed to be due to ill-treatment at home. He was put on a high-calorie diet with mineral and vitamin suplements and Calvepen tablets. His condition improved . He was discharged home on the 22nd January and an appointment was made for him to attend the Paediatric Clinic.

Yours sincerely,

Letter from hospital re Ken Doyle, 1970

AN BORD SLAINTE LAR TIRE

MIDLAND HEALTH BOARD
COUNTY HOSPITAL, TULLAMORE Phone : 21501

15th January, 1974.

Re: Kenneth Doyle, 3, Pearse Park, Tullamore.

Dear

It was thought that this child had coeliac disease and he was put on a Gluten-free diet in 1971 (November) He was brought by a sister today and she does not know much about the child and does not think that he is on a strict gluten free diet. He has only gained 1lb. in weight in the last two years. I should like to see him again if he is accompanied by his mother. He is not looking well and he should be on a gluten-free diet.

Yours sincerely,

Letter from Health Board re Ken Doyle, 1974

# Psychologist's report re Ken Doyle, 1976

MOORE ABBEY PSYCHOLOGICAL SERVI

90

Telephone: (045)25327.

Monasterevan,
Co. Kildare.

MIDLAND HEALTH BOARD
RECD
-2 FEB 1976
Ref. No.

30th January '76.

Midland Health Board,
Courthouse,
Tullamore,
Co. Offaly.

Re: Kenneth Doyle,
Pearse Park, Tullamore.

Dear ,

Kenneth Doyle presented for assessment accompanied by father. Both were late by about 1 hour and 15 minutes, consequently it was not possible to carry out a detailed cognitive evaluation.

Mr. Doyle indicated that Kenneth was born following a seven month pregnancy during which his wife was haemhorraging for a period up to the birth. His arrival at the motor and language milestones of infancy would appear to have been within the normal time periods.

Kenneth was admitted to hospital at 21 months, due to gastroenteritis which first manifested itself when he was two months old. For the first few days after his admission to hospital Kenneth's life was in the balance. He remained in hospital for six months. Mr. Doyle mentioned two other admissions to hospital, one he alleges was as a result of malnutrition. The other for the setting of a leg after an alleged fall down the stairs

. Lately his son has taken to running away from home and has on one occasion absconded from school.

Kenneth, I met for approximately an hour and took the opportunity of using a shortened form of the WISC. He presented as an extremely physically undersized, sad looking boy. He indicated he was very unhappy at home, stating that he could not

FROM ... FILES 289

say why but that he was. He showed no anxiety about the prospect of attending a boarding school. He impresses as a boy of dull to normal/average intelligence. His school work would not appear to reflect his ability. His teacher feels he cannot master school assignments, pay attention in class, relate with his peers, and his behaviour often quickly brings him to the attention of the headmaster, because of his anti-social qualities. His class teacher states that it is difficult to encapsulate the many problems this boy has. "He is a thief, a liar, and an actor."

There was some suggestion of this boy being a coeliac, though Public Health Nurse, states investigations were carried out but were found to be negative.

My impression from meeting Mr. Doyle and Kenneth was of a depressed boy whose physical and mental health has and is seriously at risk in his present environment. The onset of this child's battering, based on Mr. Doyle's allegations, would appear to have commenced when he was approximately 18 months old. Should only one twentieth of the allegations of Mr. Doyle about the abuse of Kenneth by his mother be true, he would still be seriously at risk.

As a first step I feel he should be admitted to a hospital such as Temple Street where a full paediatric work-up could be undertaken, including Xrays of all limbs, and secondly I feel the social worker should make a full evaluation of the dynamics, at the same time being very much aware that these allegations are made by Mr. Doyle who stated his wife would certainly take it out on Kenneth if there was any query about her competence.

3). Following on the social worker's report a place of safety order should be sought for Kenneth. A foster family, preferably not in the Tullamore area may be more appropriate, than a home.

Mr. Doyle would prefer contact be made through him, rather than his wife. He can be contacted at his father's house, telephone number:

Mr. Doyle has within the last twelve years lived away from home and on these occasions Kenneth was very much at risk. He feels that any absence on his part from the home Kenneth will be abused. He is extremely anxious to get him away and may be in a position to pay some of the fees of his school, should it arise. Perhaps Wilson's School in Mullingar may be worth considering.

Kenneth would, I feel, need to be referred to a child psychiatrist once away from home.

Mrs. Doyle from her husband's account comes across as a woman who might benefit by some counselling and support.

Kenneth, I feel , is in need of ~~remedial~~ immediate help. Should you require any clarification of the above please contact me.

Yours sincerely,

P.S. On placement he should be referred for educational assessment & planning

AN BORD SLÁINTE LÁR TÍRE
AN TE CH MHOR, CONTAE UA bhFAILI

MIDLAND HEALTH BOARD
COURTHOUSE,
TULLAMORE,
CO. OFFALY
Phone: 21868

REF: P.A.H. 53/2.

23rd February, 1976.

Re: Kenneth Doyle, 3, Pearse Park,
TULLAMORE.

Dear Professor,

Could you please arrange to have above-mentioned boy seen at your clinic. He is severely at risk and we wish to have a full assessment prior to placing him in a school. We hope that Mount Carmel Residential School, might accept him - pending on your recommendations.

I would be glad if you could treat case as urgent.

Yours sincerely,

Social Worker.

Temple Street Hospital,
DUBLIN, 1.

KC.

Letter from social worker re Ken Doyle, 1976

83

Mount Carmel Residentail School, 23rd February, 1976
Moate,
CO. WESTMEATH.

re/ Kenneth Doyle (12 yrs), 3, Pearse Park,
Tullamore.

Dear Sister

Further to our discussion re Kenneth Doyle, I enclose both Social and Psychological Report in order to help you decide on his suitability for your school.

He is highly at risk within the present family situation. I have made arrangements for him to have a full paediatric assessment, x-rays, etc. in Temple Street. I shall let you know the result in due course.

Yours sincerely,

SOCIAL WORKER.

Letter from social worker re Ken Doyle, 1976

66

RE/ KENNETH DOYLE, 3 PEARSE PARK, TULLAMORE.

I have been in contact with this family only in relations to present request for Kenneth's admission to Salthill.

I have spoken to who was the Social Worker involved with the family. She feels that Mrs Doyle in particular is very plausible but with time it becomes obvious that her recounting of different situations can be at variance with what actually happendd. Public Health Nurse would also agree with above

of the Tullamore Garda Station has known Kenneth for quite a few years now and he feels that Ken is one of the worst cases he has known - in particular he feels that Ken has no fear of punishment and so there are no normal deterrants effective in his case.

SOCIAL WORKER.

Letter from social worker re Ken Doyle, undated

AN BORD SLÁINTE LÁR TÍRE

AN TULACH MHOR, CONTAE UA bhFAILI

87

MIDLAND HEALTH BOARD
COURTHOUSE,
TULLAMORE,
CO. OFFALY
Phone: 21868

Feb. '76.

REF: P.A.H. 53/2.

Re: Kenneth Doyle, 12 years,
3, Pearse Park, Tullamore.

Social Report:

Kenneth is one of a family of nine (9) children - five (5) boys and four(4) girls.

Mr. Doyle is a self-employed electrician and the home is kept beautifully, with very modern equipment and conveniences.

Kenneth is a severely disturbed boy, both at home and in school.

At home, Kenneth is very disruptive and disobedient. He rums away from home when his parents threaten him and he has warned his mother that he will jump into the canal. His mother treats him very roughly and has a fixation about Kenneth. She is alleged to have starved him and mistreated him. The question re coeliac is an excuse that the mother uses as the boy has been deprived of food. His teacher told me that he eats bread from the refuse bins. He wanders around the school and the head-master has been thinking seriously about having him taken from the school as he disrupts the class.

Kenneth has been hopitalized on several occasions since his birth. He has been in Temple Street Hospital and in Cherry Orchard with gastro-entoritis.

Kenneth presents as an under-nourised, frightened little boy - under size for his age. He is a very imaginative boy and tells unrealistic stories to shock people. He is very obliging and loves to help people. He is considered a very intelligent boy by his teacher and does little projects in school which surpases his peers.

Recommendations:

1. Kenneth needs to be removed from the home environment for some time.

Health Board report re the Doyle family, 1976

SCOIL ARD-MHUIRE
LUSK
CO. DUBLIN
*Telephone: 437492/437539*

156

23rd November, 1978

Midland Health Board,
County Hospital,
Tullamore,
CO. OFFALY.

Dear

Further to our telephone conversation, I'm now writing to fill you in on the up-to-date situation in relation to Ken Doyle.

For the first few weeks of his stay here Ken's behaviour was quite disruptive and disturbed. He was very attention-seeking and frequently threatened to either run away or to kill himself.

However, after the initial few weeks he began to settle down more within the school and the staff have noted a marked improvement in his overall behaviour. It is hard to say at this point if this is a temporary change or otherwise.

Ken has been going home every three weeks. We have noticed that when he returns to the school after these weekends that he appears quite tense or upset. He will be due to go home again the weekend after next (18th December) and after that he will be at home for Christmas holidays from 22nd December until 8th January.

I called to see Mrs. Doyle on last Wednesday when I was in Tullamore. I found her attitude to Ken quite ambivalent and somewhat rejecting, and would feel that she might need the opportunity to talk through her ways of coping with Ken when he is at home. Certainly, I would be very greatful for any information you could give us on how the family relate to Ken on his weekends home.

Should you require any further information, please do not hesitate to contact me. I'll look forward to hearing from you in the near future. Many thanks for your co-operation.

Yours sincerely,

SOCIAL WORKER

Letter from social worker re Ken Doyle, 1978

28

Report. Confidential.

Re: Kenneth Doyle, 3 Pearse Park, Tullamore.

Introduction. Ken Doyle was admitted to my Family Group Unit on the 16th. April, 1977. He remained in the unit until 11th. May, 1978. Ken definately benefited from his time with us and from the treatment programme which the care staff provided. (Vide care conference reports an review reports. ) However due to lack of family support, due to family attitudes and norms undermining the caring programme, due to the failure of ongoing indepth case work with the family, in spite of very hard work and very sincere efforts by the social worker, and due to the fact that Ken was slowly realising that his parents rejection was total, a point was reached where our unit could no longer cope with Kens very disturbed behaviour and could no longer provide a treatment programme to meet his needs. Ken needs help, Ken can be helped , but the type of programme he needs can only be provided in a setting where there is a staff ratio of 1:2 and where the number in the unit is very samll, not more than five.

Aim of the Report. The aim is to help those who will now be planning a treatment programme for Ken to meet Kens present needs.

Ken Doyle is a very small 13 year old boy. During his time with us his sleeping habits and eating habits were normal. I now see Ken as a very disturbed and very damaged young boy. This disturbance and damage has been caused to some extent by his home environment, by the norms and attitudes within the family circle, by the rejection of his parents and Kens realisation of this rejection, and by the unhealthy athmosphere which exists within the home. Having lived with Ken for over a year I would suggest that Ken has alos got some deep seated personal psychiatric problems. I would suggest that these need to be investigated in depth. It should be noted that his brother has been in a psychiatric hospital and is receiving treatment. Kens disturbance and damage manifasted itself within the unit as follows.

1. He was unable to form any real relationships. His relationships were of the what-can -I -get -out -of -it , mould. This was true of relations with staff and children.

2. He found it very difficult to communicate. Councelling sessions , both formal and informal by staff failed to evoke any real communication. He certainly talked a lot, he had a lot of 'chatter' but no real communication. He certainly expressed his feelings. These were feelings of rage, fustration, insecuritty, and anger. He seldom expressed feelings of warmth, tenderness, sympathy, or love.

3. His moods were unpredictable. One minute he was 'charming', the next he was violent, and abusive.

4. He was unable to cope with authority or with structured situations.

5. His fustration ceiling was very low.

6. He lied , cheated, stole, and bullied.

7. He seldom expressed guilt feelings.

8. He had all kinds of psychosomatic pains and sickness. Headaches,

Report on Ken Doyle, undated

63

page two....../

Kenneth is going home on Saturday next. The social worker will see Ken on a regualr basis during his holiday. She will also get more involved with the Doyle family with a view to future planning and support both for Ken and the rest of the family. If problems do arise Ken will be seen at the Child Guidance Clinic in Tullamore. The family will be asked firmly to accept responsibility for Ken during the holidays and how they cope will give some indication of how much responsibility they can accept and may highlight some of the basic problems within the home.

Summary.

1. Kenneth has made very good progress. He is happy , contented and secure. Getting on well in school. St. Josephs has helped him to grow as a person.
2. The home and family situation is the root cause of Kenneths problems.
3. The social worker will become more involved with the family with a view to sorting out some of the problems.
4. The social worker will see Ken on a regular basis when he is on holidays.
5. The family will be told that if Kenneth presents a problem they will have to cope. They just cant sent him back to St. Josephs as soon as a problem appears. This should help the social worker. She will be able to monotor the 'family capacity' and they may be more willing to accept her help.

AN BORD SLÁINTE LÁR TIRE
AN TULACH MHOR, CONTAE UA bhFAIL

91

MIDLAND HEALTH BOARD
Health Centre, Arden Road, XXXXXXXXXX
TULLAMORE,
CO. OFFALY
Phone: XXXX 41301.

Ken is considered to be about average in school. He will possibly do six or seven subjects in his group this year. His favourite subjects are art and crafts and cooking.

felt that Ken could possibly do an Anco course in cooking next year, as he was full of enthusiam for it. Generally he felt that Ken was getting a lot out of Lusk and that his self achievement had gone up immensely in the past year.

I explained that the home situation appeared very well at the moment, and that mother is now full of praise for Ken. However, this is likely to erupt the moment Ken steps out of line. Ken now goes home every 3 weeks. Apart from holidays and staff felt that he was always trying to buy parents affection by bringing them home objects he had made. He rarely talks about his family and sees this as Ken's way of handling the situation. I explained mother's rejection of Lusk and her constant demand that Ken never mention Lusk or boys within it. felt that I could talk to Ken about this and help him to understand mother's attitude.

Summary:

1. Kenneth has made good progress and Lusk has helped him to grow as a person.

2. Social Work involvement in the family with a view to helping mother accept Ken more.

Social Worker.

KC.

Letter from social worker re Ken Doyle, undated

# Case History, Patrick Doyle, 1969

DOYLE: Patrick.
3, Pearse Park,
Tullamore, Co. Offaly.

History taken: by Miss A Coyle on 31/10/1969

42

Patrick, aged ten-and-a-half, was referred by County Medical Officer, Offaly, because of anti-social behaviour He was reported to have taken a watch from a club in the town an also to have stolen money at home on several occasions. He is also reported to be untruthful. The history was given by Mr. Doyle who has a rather florid complexion and is a well-spoken ma in his forties. He was uncertain and unsure of himself in the interviewing situation and mentioned in the beginning that he ha taken a few drinks in order to come to the Clinic today with Patrick. (The exact date of Patrick's birth is not known as this time.)

Patrick is the second-eldest in a family of seven. He is a pupil in 5th Class in Tullamore National School.

Problem

Mr. Doyle feels that Patrick is a good child and that the m difficulty at home is that his wife has little or no time for Patrick or for his five-year old brother, Kenneth. She "has something against them". It appears that Patrick has to do all the housework at home, such as making the beds. While his fathe is away from home, she will give him nothing to eat; as a result he has stolen money from her in order to buy food during the wee In 1965 Mr. Doyle's parents contacted the I.S.P.C.C. in Athlone because Patrick was obviously hungry and was taking food out of the neighbouring bins. At that time, Mr. Doyle, who is an electrical contractor, was working away from home and was unaware of the fact that his wife was not feeding Patrick. He has gone to the Priests on one or two occasions to ask them to talk to his wife, but they would not come to his home and his wife refused to go to the Priests. Mr. Doyle was insistent that in other areas his wife is a very good mother and is good to the other five children, but, with Patrick and Kenneth, she insists that they are bad and that they are going to be bad, and, when she learned-

learned/

42 that Patrick was coming up to the Child Guidance Clinic to-day, she spent yesterday telling him he was mad and that he would be put away. It reached the point where the child became hysterical and refused to move out of the home. Mr. Doyle is also concerned about Kenneth, aged five, whom he said is wasting away and is nothing but skin and bones. He also gets nothing to eat when his father is out of the home. Mrs. Doyle gets the older children to follow Patrick and Kenneth to school to make sure that they dont go into a shop or call into their grandparents to get food on the way to and from school.

At school, Patrick is doing very well and is considered to be of average intelligence and he enjoys going to school. Kenneth also started school this year. They both play well and have good relations with other children; they also get along with their siblings.

Mr. Doyle describes himself as being from a well-to-do family and says that he himself is successful in his business and that money is no object at all. He cannot understand why his wife will not spend money on these two children.

Mrs. Doyle is from Dublin; she is one of six children. Her mother died when she was young and she was raised by her elder sister. Her father worked in C.I.E. Prior to her marriage she worked in Players' factory in Phibsboro. She has settled down in Tullamore and likes it there although she does not mix with the neighbours. She does not talk to her husband's family as they come down on her for the way she treats the children. Mr. Doyle described her as being a very good wife and a good mother, and was reluctant to say that there was anything wrong with the marriage. However, it was evident from talking with him that all has not been well for some time.

I talked with Mr. Doyle about the importance of both children being seen. He agreed with this and felt that if he could get the children to a boarding school that this would help the situation.

situation./

42 He does not see his wife accepting any plans that we may have. He was reluctant to say that his wife might need help. He feels that if he has to suggest this that his wife will start a fight and, if this happens, he will leave home. However, he is certain that he is going to do something about these two chilren, even if it means going against his wife. I asked him to talk to about referring Kenneth and that he should come up the next time that Patrick comes. He agreed to do this and to return also in the meantime himself.

Impression

Mr. Doyle appears to be a dependent, passive man who is reluctant to take any initiative or action. He will need a lot of support in order to bring both the children here. The situation at home has continued and he has been aware of it, at least, since 1965 when the I.S.P.C.C. were called in and it is only now that he is beginning to do something about it. I feel it would be important to keep a close contact with Mr. Doyle and the two boys at this point.

OFFALY COUNTY COUNCIL 40

PUBLIC HEALTH DEPARTMENT
COURTHOUSE
TULLAMORE

REF........................

9th January, 1970.

Hospitaller Order of St. John of God,
Child Guidance Clinic,
Orwell Road,
Rathgar,
Dublin.

Re:- Patrick Doyle, 3, Pearse Park,
Tullamore, your ref: 753/10/222.

Dear Brother

The abovementioned attended the Child Guidance Clinic on 21/11/1969 and to date I have not received a report. Will you kindly let me have a report.

Psychiatric Social Worker at the Clinic rang to-day and she informed me that she wishes Patrick to attend again and also his brother Kenneth. Apparently the father mentioned about Kenneth when he attended with Patrick on 21st November.

I have requested the father to let me know if he will agree to bring Patrick and Kenneth to the clinic if appointments are made and I will write to you again if he agrees.

Yours sincerely.

County M.O.

SH.

14th February 1975.

Midland Health Board.

Re: Patrick Doyle, 3 Pearse Park, Tullamore

Dear Dr. ,

I am asking Brother Secretary to enclose copies of reports on Patrick Doyle. I last saw Patrick two years ago when he was facing a Court charge because of some anti-social event. You will see that he is a dull but not mentally handicapped, anti-social boy who appears to have rejected for some reason or another from early childhood.

ENCLOSURES

THIS FILE STATES THAT PATRICK WAS REJECTED FROM EARLY CHILDHOOD

Doctor's note re Patrick Doyle, 1975

25

Born: 2/7/58

4th Sept. 1972.

Patrick Doyle, 3, Pearse Park, Tullamore.
C.M.O., Midland Health Board, Offaly.

Patrick was not accompanied by either parents so that we do not know how he is progressing as he, as usual, was very optimistic about life and he denies having any problems at all.

I do hope that his mother can come the next day as the main difficulty lies in his relationship with her and it would be important for her to come to see our Social Worker while I see Patrick.

I would like to see him again in four weeks' time.

Medical Director.

Doctor's note re Patrick Doyle, 1972

**MIDLAND HEALTH BOARD**

I hereby consent to myself

having a course of Electroconvulsive Therapy. I realise that there are certain dangers involved.

SIGNED: × Patrick Doyle

DATE: 19/3/76

---

Psychiatric Hospital consent form agreeing to electroshock therapy signed by Patrick Doyle, 1976

FOR CASE PAPER FILE

..................... No.

# PATIENT'S PRIVATE PROPERTY RECORD SHEET

Name of Patient: Paddy Doyle Reg. No. ..........................................

Address: Tullamore, Pearse Pk. Date of Admission: 19/3/76.

SCHEDULE OF PROPERTY BROUGHT INTO THE HOSPITAL BY THE ABOVE-NAMED ON ADMISSION

Signed: .................................... Date: 19/3/76

Witnessed: ....................................

| CLOTHING | | JEWELLERY | | MISCELLANEOUS ITEMS | | CASH, ETC. |
|---|---|---|---|---|---|---|
| 1 jumper | | | | | | |
| 1 jeans | | | | | | |
| 1 shirt | | | | | | |
| 1 socks. | | | | | | |
| 1 overcoat | | | | | | |
| 1 shoes | | | | | | |
| | | | | | | |
| | | | | | | |
| | | | | | | |
| | | | | | | |

RECEIVED:

.......................... .......................... .......................... ..........................

...ions Printing Works.

Patrick Doyle's Patient Private Property Record Sheet from psychiatric hospital, 1976

# It Shouldn't Hurt to be a Child

If you are being abused or you suspect that a child is being abused, or neglected, please contact the Irish Society for the Prevention of Cruelty to Children (ISPCC) on (01) 676 7960. (www.ispcc.ie) The ISPCC provides a 24-hour-a-day, 7-days-a-week listening service for children called Childline. You can phone them on 1800 666 666. (www.childline.ie)

You can also contact the Children's Rights Alliance at 4 Upper Mount Street, Dublin 2. Their number is (01) 662 9400. (www.childrensrights.ie)

In the USA the National Child Abuse Hotline is 1-800-422-4453 (www.childhelp.org)

In the UK you can call the National Society for the Prevention of Cruelty to Children on 0808 800 5000.
You can also call the NSPCC's ChildLine service on 0800 11 11. (www.nspcc.org.uk)

www.obrien.ie